SECRET
SAN FRANCISCO

SECRET
SAN FRANCISCO

The Unique Guidebook to San Francisco's Hidden Sites, Sounds, & Tastes

David Armstrong

WITH PHOTOGRAPHS BY
Linda Rutenberg

ECW PRESS

The publication of *Secret San Francisco* has been generously supported by the Canada Council, the Ontario Arts Council, and the Government of Canada through the Book Publishing Industry Development Program.

NATIONAL LIBRARY OF CANADA CATALOGUING IN PUBLICATION DATA

Armstrong, David, 1945-
Secret San Francisco: the unique guidebook to San Francisco's hidden sites, sounds & tastes
Includes index.
ISBN 1-55022-438-7
1. San Francisco (Calif.) – Guidebooks. I. Title.
F869.S33A76 2001   917.94'610454   C00-933279-0

Original series design by Paul Davies, ECW Type and Art, Oakville, Ontario.
Typesetting by Martel *en-tête*.
Imaging and cover by Guylaine Régimbald – SOLO DESIGN.
Printed by Printcrafters, Winnipeg, Manitoba, Canada.

Distributed in Canada by General Distribution Services,
325 Humber College Boulevard, Etobicoke, Ontario M9W 7C3.

Distributed in the United States by LPC Group,
1436 West Randolph Street, Chicago, Illinois, U.S.A. 60607.

Published by ECW PRESS
2120 Queen Street East, Suite 200, Toronto, Ontario M4E 1E2.

ecwpress.com

PRINTED AND BOUND IN CANADA

TABLE OF CONTENTS

Introduction

How to Use *Secret San Francisco*

SECRET . . .

For Blair, who is no secret.

INTRODUCTION

San Francisco is two cities: the pretty tourist mecca of glossy travel brochures, and the layered, flawed, intoxicating city that San Franciscans actually live in. Both cities exist, but one is more interesting than the other. This is a book for travelers who want to go beyond the postcard photo-ops and the tried and untrue tourist destinations, and explore the vibrant neighborhoods, intimate hideaways, and out-there adventures that make San Francisco so much more than pretty.

This book was written to help you explore the city, encourage you to lose yourself in it, and come to know it the way the locals do. In the process, you may fall in love with San Francisco — many do — but your love won't be blind.

In *Secret San Francisco*, I tell you how to take a walk on the city's extreme-and-proud-of-it wild side with a pretty fair expectation of coming back intact. Tourist traps? San Francisco has plenty. I level with you about them and tell you where to find secret treasures buried in the tackiest of traps. Wondering where you can do your laundry after days of touring and partying? I point you to places where you can chill out with California craft beers while you put your clothes in another kind of suds.

Appropriately for a city with the most restaurants per capita in the United States, this book begins with Secret All You Can Eat and ends with Secret Wine. Come with me to San Francisco's most elegant expense-account Valhallas, to its no-frills, ultra-cheap joints, and to its multicultural delights. I show you an ice cream parlor where you can savor cardamom and saffron rose flavors, and a unique bistro where you can swim without shame in the glorious grease and pillowing starch of white-trash food.

One more thing: I also tell you where to find the rarest commodity of all in a compact city clogged with suvs and pickup trucks on steroids — a parking space.

HOW TO USE
SECRET SAN FRANCISCO

This book is arranged alphabetically by subject. If you love the blues, go to the Secret Blues section. If you relish Japanese food, flip the pages till you get to Secret Japanese. Should you yearn to try something new — say, Taiwanese pearl drinks — read all about it under that very heading.

For every business, there is a telephone number and street address; all phone numbers are in the 415 area code unless otherwise noted. This is a city-centric book, but when there is a can't-miss, gotta-go attraction outside the city limits, I give you the word. The book doesn't give directions, prices, or hours of operation unless something about them really stands out — I figure you're resourceful enough to call ahead. And you should. Since the dot-com revolution erupted in the mid-1990s, commercial development in San Francisco has been on fast forward, with businesses being born and dying like flies.

For updates and more detail than I can offer here, be sure to check the Secret Periodicals section. It lists print publications and Web sites that provide fast-changing information about an ever-changing city.

SECRET

ALL YOU CAN EAT

You feel as though you've dined in all 3,000 San Francisco restaurants and dropped a bundle in most of them, especially the industrial-chic destination restaurants where the airplane-like noise levels kept your partner from reminding you how much all this was costing. What to do? Fear not, Famished One. The city has a deep supply of places where you can chow down to your heart's content for one set price. If you choose well, you can make a groaning-board lunch or dinner your main meal of the day, and it needn't be a budget buster.

Many Indian restaurants offer all-you-can-eat buffet lunches. San Francisco will never rival London for the variety, number, and quality of Indian places, but the buffets offer good value and feature popular items from the standard menu — though some sit on the steam table too long. If you're downtown, check out the **New Delhi Restaurant and Bar** (160 Ellis St., 397-8470), a cavernous place with portraits of 19th-century maharajahs and a framed photo of a smiling Bill Clinton making a phone call from the restaurant. The New Delhi offers a fixed-price steam-table buffet with good tandoori chicken, lentils in gravy, a buttery rice pudding, spicy zucchini, cauliflower dishes, and other items that change daily. Elsewhere in town, Indian eateries with similar fare include **India Clay Oven** (2435 Clement St., 751-0505) and **Natraj Indian Restaurant** (5217 Geary Blvd., 831-7898) in the Richmond, and **Ganesh** (2700 16th St., 437-9240) in the Mission. Ganesh is cheaper than most, and Natraj is even cheaper; its weekend buffet lunch goes for $3.99.

All-you-can-eat meals are common at other ethnic eateries, as well.

Coriya Hot Pot City (852 Clement St., 387-7888) in the inner Richmond serves up savory Chinese hot pot food and barbeque. You bring the food from a raw bar and cook it yourself at your table, seasoning to taste. This is a shiny, busy place that always seems to be humming; it's popular with small groups of locals, who line up outside. There must be at least two of you to order the all-you-can-eat special, which applies to dinner and lunch.

If Korean barbeque is to your liking, you can eat yourself silly at **Shabu Shabu** (1375 Ninth Ave., 661-7879). Does all the sushi you can absorb sound good? Try **Natori** (327 Balboa St., 387-2565), a Japanese restaurant with a seafood buffet. East African? Check out the buffet lunch at **New Eritrea** (907 Irving Ave., 681-1288) for Eritrean and Ethiopian fare. Try the zigni, squares of beef simmered in red pepper sauce and spices, and wash them down with imported Ethiopian beers like Hakim Lager. Sit in the bright back courtyard under the skylight, far from the blaring TV set in the main dining room.

But suppose all this internationalism is wearing thin, and you hanker for a good old American spread. No problem, Mac. Try the Sunday afternoon all-you-can-eat barbeque at **Bottom of the Hill** (1233 17th St., 621-4455), one of the city's hippest music clubs-cum-bars. The fleshy feed of burger, dogs, and chicken starts at 4 p.m. Sundays (if the place isn't booked for a party — call first), followed by live music at 5 p.m., both on the same ticket. Beginning at 5 p.m. on Mondays, in the same Potrero Hill 'hood as Bottom of the Hill, **Goat Hill Pizza** (300 Connecticut St., 641-1440) offers all the pizza and salad you can eat. Servers bring out the pizza a slice at a time; you troll the salad bar yourself. This is standard-issue American pizza, minus most of the trendy toppings at pricier places. Nothing fancy, but it's tasty and sustaining.

SECRET
ARCHITECTURE

Before I tell you about the grand, impressive, beautiful buildings that abound in San Francisco, I want to tell you about smallish, improvisational, whimsical pieces that blend architecture and art, and convey the spirit of the city. They're temporary, so do see them first; ornate, historic City Hall will still be there when you're ready.

Don't miss the old brick building on the southwest corner of heavily trafficked Howard and Sixth streets. You'll see dozens of chairs, tables, lamps, a bed, and other furniture attached to the exterior walls at rakish angles. Why are they there? I dunno. What does it mean? Probably nothing. But it's fun, and it lets you see a dreary Skid Row intersection with new eyes; maybe that's enough.

At nearby **689 and 691 Minna Street**, a yellow Victorian duplex sports a metal sculpture of the world on its roof. Outside the second floor is a large twisted-metal cage in the shape of a fish, hovering over the sidewalk. It provides unexpected pleasure on Minna, a skinny alley just south of Mission Street. Just east of the globe house on Minna is a parking lot, beyond which you glimpse the neighborhood's traditional architecture: sun-bleached wooden decks and funky, back-of-the-house wooden stairs. A lot of cooking out and hanging out goes on in such places, off the city's alleys. Maybe someone will invite you up.

San Francisco is famous for its Victorians: highly decorative, brightly painted wooden houses put up as private homes between 1860 and 1920. Many burned down in the great earthquake and fire of 1906, and many others were torn down to make way for dubious urban

renewal. However, there are still 14,000 Victorians left, in Italianate, Queen Anne, and other ornate styles. The most-photographed Victorian site is postcard row, six houses on Steiner Street that form a quaint foreground with skyscrapers towering in the background. Groves of Victorians sprout on Buena Vista West Avenue and elsewhere around the Haight-Ashbury, as well as in Pacific Heights, where crowds are generally sparser. For an interior view, you can tour the fabulously over-the-top **Haas-Lilenthal House** (2007 Franklin St., 441-3004), a restored 1886 gingerbread mansion with period furnishings.

San Francisco is not as well known for its Art Moderne gems, but they are sleekly entertaining and, unlike the justly famous Victorians, seldom have tour groups out front.

One of my favorites is the **Malloch Apartment Building** (1360 Montgomery St.), a 1937 Art Moderne structure perched on the east side of Telegraph Hill. The apartments were featured in the 1946 Humphrey Bogart flick *Dark Passage*; today, a big cardboard cutout of Bogie overlooks the street from an apartment window. Adorning the outside walls are smoothly stylized deco images of birds, ships, bridges, and a man hoisting a giant globe.

Scarcely less ambitious is another of my faves, the 1929 office building at **450 Sutter Street**. Chiefly a warren of doctors' offices, 450 Sutter has a great gold façade around a grand entrance, etched with mysterious squiggles that look like the product of an Aztec Rosicrucian designer on acid. Take a look inside, and survey the elaborate decorative touches by the elevators and on the walls, the ceilings, and the floors.

While you're downtown, take a look at the **Hallidie Building** (130 Sutter St.). A 1917 creation, it has the world's first glass curtain wall, a large and lovely structure flanked by a cast-iron cornice and fire escapes that architect Willis Polk intended to resemble drapes and a window pull. For more stylistic flourishes, see the **Folk Art International Gallery** (140 Maiden Lane), a 1911 building remodeled in 1949 by Frank Lloyd Wright. It features a brick archway over the front door and an interior spiral staircase that Wright later replicated on a larger scale in New York's Guggenheim Museum.

Also downtown, right across the street from one another, are the **Russ Building** (235 Montgomery St.), a 1927 structure with an arched doorway and marble interior, and the **Mills Building** (220 Montgomery St.), a Romanesque Revival landmark built in 1891. Down the street is the exquisite **Hong Kong Trade and Economic Office Building** (130 Montgomery St.), a restored 1930 Art Moderne gem. Dwarfed by its neighbors, this six-story building has a delicate beauty that makes it stand out.

Even business centers that are largely off limits to the public often have spectacular lobbies. This is especially true of major banks. Check out the ultra-high, gold-colored ceilings of the Crocker branch of **Wells Fargo Bank** at 1 Montgomery Street and the **Bank of America** at the cable car turnaround (1 Powell St.).

Now you're ready for **City Hall** (200 Polk St., 554-4000). Built in 1915 and closed from 1994 to 1999 for a $300-million seismic upgrade and restoration, this Beaux Arts palace re-opened to rave reviews. The grand marble staircase in the great rotunda has witnessed lavish parties, ceremonies, and parades of newlyweds for generations (among the latter, Marilyn Monroe and S.F. homeboy Joe DiMaggio). The rotunda is topped by a great dome, rather cheekily raised higher than the dome over the U.S. Capitol. For the best view of the rotunda, go to the fourth floor and peer down. Chiseled into the wall is this inspirational reference to the great earthquake and fire of 1906: "San

Francisco, O glorious city of our hearts, that has been tried and not found wanting, go thou with like spirit to make the future thine."

Stolid Beaux Arts buildings border the Civic Center, along with the 1996 **Main Library** (100 Larkin St., 557-4400). Architecturally, the library is a mish-mash of styles, but its light-flooded atrium is impressive. An evocative artwork, *Untitled*, girds the walls between the third and fifth floors with 50,000 hand-notated catalog cards from the old, pre-computerized main library.

San Francisco is a city of eccentrics, so it seems fitting to end my shortlist of must-see buildings with a house inspired by a great American character. That would be the 1861 **Octagon House** (2645 Gough St., 441-7512), an eight-sided structure built along lines popularized by phrenologist Orson Fowler. As well as asserting that character and health could be predicted by feeling the bumps of the head, Fowler — a New York publisher who issued Walt Whitman's *Leaves of Grass* — argued that people could improve their health by dwelling in harmoniously proportioned octagons. Meticulously restored by the Colonial Dames of America, the house — health-giving or not — looks splendid and is open for tours.

If you're really dedicated to architecture, go to the Visitors Center in **Hallidie Plaza** (Powell and Market) and grab the free *Art to Architecture* brochure, part of the San Francisco Convention and Visitors Bureau's Diverse City series. The brochure details up to five full days of self-guided tours, complete with public transit and walking directions. If you need more after that, may I recommend a 12-step program for recovering architecture junkies?

SECRET
BEACHES

For travelers unfamiliar with temperate San Francisco, it must be said (and it cannot be said too often): this city is not in southern California, home of palm trees, monster surfing, beach bunnies, hot weather, and beach culture in general. No. It is located in northern California, where winds and the Pacific waters are much cooler than down in SoCal and where ocean swimming is apt to be a chilly challenge, even in the warmest months (which are, incidentally, September and October).

That said, San Francisco has several interesting beaches. The largest is Ocean Beach, the most beautiful is Baker Beach, and the most secluded and atmospheric is China Beach. All are located on the west side of town fronting the Pacific Ocean. San Francisco Bay, to the east and north, bristles with old finger piers, parks, shopping malls, waterfront restaurants and bars, marinas, and shipyards, as well as Pacific Bell Park and a gorgeous pedestrian promenade (all are covered in other sections of this book), but not beaches.

Ocean Beach, which runs north and south for three miles flanked by the romantically named Great Highway, is the biggest and wildest city beach — both for its rough surf, braved by surfer dudes and dudettes in wetsuits, and for its parties. Ocean Beach gave rise to Burning Man, the Generation X music and art festival designed to put you in touch with your inner pagan. When the beach became too small for the growing gathering, Burning Man was moved far away from the ocean: to the desert, in fact, where admission will run you $200. But you can still get a taste of the early days of Burning Man,

for free, at the **Burning Man Beach Burn** (www.burningman.com) on the last Saturday of each month. Head to Ocean Beach stairway 28, between Fulton and Lincoln streets; things get started about 8 p.m. Bring your own food and drink, and artwork to burn. There's dancing. There's drumming. There's the climactic bonfire.

China Beach, named for the 19th-century Chinese men who fished there, is the smallest city beach and one highly prized by locals. Located just off El Camino del Mar near 26th Avenue, the strand lies at the foot of the cliff. You can reach it by going down a macadam ramp (closed to cars) or a dirt stairway firmed up with wooden frames. A deco structure used by the Beach Patrol also houses decrepit locker rooms, rest rooms, and showers. The sand beach is very small and lightly visited; on a day when Baker Beach had hundreds of frolicking visitors, I counted six beachcombers at China Beach. It's easy to forget you are in a big city here. The place is a bracing reminder that San Francisco once owed its existence to the sea.

Baker Beach, located at the end of Bowley Street, off Lincoln Boulevard in the Presidio, is flat-out gorgeous. There's ample free parking and a public strand bordered by restored, fenced-off sand dunes with native California grasses. Off to your right as you gaze out to sea is a stunning view of the Golden Gate Bridge. If you walk toward the bridge, following the path, you will find a smallish patch of Baker Beach dedicated to nude sunbathing; it's on a bit of land just west of the noble bridge, one of the world's great manmade objects.

Incidentally, North Beach, known for Beat writers and Italian cafes, has no beach. Bayfill — our version of landfill — obliterated the original shoreline years ago.

S E C R E T

BEADS

I never thought I was interested in beads — in fact, I never thought about beads at all, being non-decorative enough to verge on the Puritan — until I visited the aptly named **General Bead** (637 Minna St., 621-8187). Tucked away on a trashy, occasionally smelly block of Minna, an alley just south of Mission Street, General Bead occupies two floors of a vintage building. Inside, the place rocks. When I first walked in, James Brown was playing on the sound system, and staffers with blonde dreadlocks and nose rings were zipping around. Bags and bags of beads — from the Czech Republic, Japan, and multitudinous other places — are displayed in boxes on the walls. Behind the counter, numbered bins contain retail and wholesale items. In addition to beads of all colors, sizes, and prices, General Bead sells earrings, butterfly hairclips, and other stuff. But mostly it sells beads.

Upstairs, the shop is lined with campy old movie posters for the likes of *Candy, I Am Curious (Yellow),* and *Hitchhike to Hell,* and there's a small roomful of beaded curtains. Downstairs, customers tread an aquamarine floor dusted with sparkles and place their orders while standing on a giant flower. A handwritten note explains why the friendly but hard-working staff uses the flower method: "Please go to the flower on the floor marked 'Stand here for help.' Your cooperation with 'standing on the flower' helps us to serve you more quickly and with less confusion. If someone asks you to stand on the flower, please don't take it personally. We are just trying to keep things pleasant and fair for everybody." Noted.

Across town, in North Beach, funky energy gives way to Zen calm at **Yone SF** (478 Union St., 986-1424), where proprietor Hermon Baker sells "beads, jewelry, and treasures" (but not finished beadwork). It is smaller, pricier, and quieter than General Bead. Yone, which sells beads made from rare materials, has a fine chandelier and shines with refinement. Baker says he has been in business "forever." Given Yone's air of timeless contemplation, that seems eminently plausible.

SECRET
BEATS
❦

It all begins with **City Lights Bookstore** (261 Columbus Ave., 362-8193). The first all-paperback bookshop in America when it opened in 1953, City Lights was and is a beacon for admirers of Beat literature: people seeking admission to Coney Islands of the mind, people living on the road, people howling in the wilderness of an often-indifferent society.

The existence of this bookstore (City Lights is also a publisher) is no secret, of course. In some circles, it's legendary. But the secret of its longevity and enduring influence may be simply that City Lights hasn't wavered from its commitment to ferocious independence. City Lights still champions critical thinking and the writer's voice. It sells and publishes works by the Beats — Allen Ginsberg, Jack Kerouac, William S. Burroughs, co-founder and co-owner Lawrence Ferlinghetti, and more — but doesn't limit itself to the Beat canon. New writing makes its way onto the store's bookshelves and periodicals rack, one of the city's best.

City Lights displays new and classic books (there are now hard covers as well as paperbacks) in street side windows, and black and white photos from the 1950s and '60s; my photo pick is a shot of Bob Dylan, Ginsberg, and poet Michael McClure, all looking wiry and alert, ready for the next thing. Inside, the store rambles and spills over three levels; it has expanded in stages over the years and was named a city landmark in 2000. A year earlier, Ferlinghetti, who still works in the upstairs office, bought the building with business partner Nancy J. Peters — sparing it from redevelopment, one hopes.

A narrow, twisting stairway leads to the basement, where a section on Native American history is labeled Stolen Continents, another section is labeled Commodity Esthetics, and other sections house books about jazz, anarchism, and political theory. After half a century, City Lights retains its quirky particularity in an age of metastasizing chains.

Directly across Jack Kerouac Alley from City Lights is another place intimately linked to the Beats and still going strong. **Vesuvio Cafe** (255 Columbus Ave., 362-3370), despite being called a cafe, is a bar, and a great one. The Beats drank here. So can you. Co-owner Janet Clyde is a sparky, friendly presence behind the plank. Nothing could be finer than to climb the stairs to Vesuvio's mezzanine with a quality paperback and a pint of Anchor Steam beer, San Francisco's premium amber brew, and take a window seat, occasionally looking out at the parade of people and cars on Columbus.

Other sites linked to the Beats can be found — many in altered form — in North Beach, the Italian neighborhood that drew the Beats west from New York in the late 1940s and 1950s with cheap rents and a tolerant atmosphere. The tolerant atmosphere lives on. Not so the cheap rents.

The **Co-Existence Bagel Shop** (1398 Grant Ave.), a haunt for Beat poets and friends, such as the writer Richard Brautigan, is now a video store. **The Place** (1546 Grant Ave.), a hangout and site for poetry readings and rants, is now a private design studio; look for the big plaster dog in the window. **Gino & Carlo** (548 Green St., 421-0896), an unpretentious neighborhood bar where the Beats liked to drink and eat, is still an unpretentious neighborhood bar where locals like to drink and eat; it doesn't play up its connection to the Beats. The **Coffee Gallery** (1353 Grant Ave.), a jazz and poetry venue where the brilliant monologist Lord Buckley performed, is now the **Lost and Found Saloon**, a no-frills bar with the prow of a boat serving as a table; Kerouac and fellow adventurer Neal Cassady would fit right in. Ginsberg's residence at 1010 Montgomery Street, where he wrote his breakthrough poem "Howl," survives as a well-kept apartment building on the corner of Montgomery and Broadway.

Should you wish to stick around, you can try the **Hotel Boheme** (444 Columbus Ave., 433-9111), a reasonably priced retreat in a green and cream vintage building, with Beat memorabilia on the walls and a no-smoking policy.

SECRET
BEER

People think of San Francisco as a wine and cocktail town, and it is, but it's also a beer town. The American brewpub movement, which started across the bay in Hayward in the 1980s, has since flowered in San Francisco, too. A great local brewery, Anchor Brewing Company, was revived in the 1960s, and terrific local bars pour craft beers made close to home and around the world. Of the dozen brewpubs in S.F., the best are Thirsty Bear Brewing Company, San Francisco Brewing

Company, Magnolia Pub & Brewery, and Beach Chalet Brewery & Restaurant.

Thirsty Bear (661 Howard St., 974-0905), located a wobbly walk away from the Moscone Convention Center, is a big, converted industrial space whose hard surfaces bounce sound around. So it's noisy. But, hey, it's a bar. Thirsty Bear is a scene after work, with beautiful things elbowing up to the bar and grazing on the unique, very tasty Catalan tapas. There are pool tables and darts upstairs, with dining tables and the bar downstairs. You'll find seven beers on tap, including a clean, crisp, blonde wheat beer.

San Francisco Brewing Company (155 Columbus Ave., 434-3344) is smallish, crowded, and convivial. Lunches and dinners are passable, but the real attraction is the relaxed ambience: the pub sets out sidewalk tables and chairs on nice days on its corner site, where North Beach, the financial district, and Chinatown meet. The excellent Emperor Norton lager is named for a 19th-century S.F. character, who issued his own scrip to merchants. They accepted it, allowing him to dine and shop free. A few pints, and you'll be a character, too.

Magnolia (1398 Haight St., 864-PINT) occupies the ground floor of a Victorian building at the happening corner of Haight and Masonic. It serves an eclectic menu featuring the likes of green onion rice fritters and ale-steamed mussels, and pours outstanding ales and beers. Some of Magnolia's ales are conditioned in casks and hand pumped, and these are especially toothsome. Blue Bell Bitter and other brews reveal a British influence, but Magnolia is not a British pub. It's just very good, arguably the city's best.

The Beach Chalet (1000 Great Hwy., 386-8439) makes good pilsner, ale, and porter, and serves food a notch above standard pub grub. It's in a beautiful spot, a beachfront 1920s Willis Polk-designed building with a second-floor view of the Pacific, and 1930s murals on the first floor. The Beach Chalet is busy and noisy; try to go early or late. It's a fine place to watch the sunset with a glass of pilsner in hand or to groove to live music on weekends — especially in winter, when storms blow in from the ocean and lash the windows.

Other great beer bars, though they don't make their own, include **The Bitter End** (441 Clement St., 221-9538), which serves Irish and British imports, and features understandably "Manic Mondays," when draft beers are $2.50 all night; **Toronado** (547 Haight St., 863-2276), which has 40-plus beers on tap, including German brews like Bitburger, in punked-out digs; and the **Pig & Whistle** (2801 Geary Blvd., 885-4779), a haunt for University of San Francisco students and older imbibers, with a good selection of draft and bottled beers, and a pool room. **Walzwerk** (381 S. Van Ness Ave., 551-7181) is an East German restaurant with hard-to-find German beers on tap. Look for the portraits of Marx and Engels on the wall above the metal tables and chairs.

Definitely the most novel place in town to drink beer is **Brain Wash Cafe/Laundromat** (1122 Folsom St., 431-WASH). The coin laundry is open until 1 a.m. Fridays and Saturdays; there's also a washing and folding service. The cafe offers at least half a dozen rotating craft beers on tap, as well as light meals and snacks. It all helps you while away the time while your clothes finish the rinse cycle. You can check out the bulletin board for notices about upcoming spoken-word and poetry events, and gigs by local bands, or use one of the computers to go online.

If you want to see how great beers are made — Liberty Ale, Anchor Steam beer, and Old Foghorn barley wine, among them — reserve a place on one of the free tours of **Anchor Brewing** (1705 Mariposa St., 863-8350), which take place each weekday at 2 p.m. Raise a toast to washing machine heir Fritz Maytag; he saved Anchor from going under by buying it in the 1960s, then greatly improved and diversified the product.

If you want a six-pack or big bottles of hard-to-find beers, pay a visit to **Liberty Market** (23rd Ave. at Geary Blvd., no listed phone), which claims to have the best beer selection in town, with 350 brands. I haven't counted them, but suffice it to say the beer fridge takes up one entire side of the shop. If you're going out of town and fancy a different pub experience, try the **Ace in the Hole** (3100 Gravenstein Hwy. N., Sebastopol, 707-829-1101), a cheery Sonoma County place run by an expatriate Brit that makes its own hard cider. It's the first all-cider pub in the United States.

SECRET
BICYCLES

Sorry about the hills. San Francisco's topography makes it tough for all but the most seasoned riders to handle the much-photographed hills and dales around here. But don't despair! There are beautiful, and beautifully flat, places to ride elsewhere in the city, most notably along the waterfront and in Golden Gate Park, which undulates ever so gently.

San Francisco has an official transit-first policy, by which it means to challenge the supremacy of the automobile. Although this policy is often more honored in the breach than in the observance, the city has encouraged cyclists by marking bike lanes on city streets and posting route signs. If the signs bear orange graphics, it's a cross-town route; if the graphics are green and white, it's a neighborhood route. Much

of the **San Francisco Bicycle Program** (www.ci.sf.ca.us/dpt/) is aimed at commuters, but it can be helpful to visitors, too.

Unless you brought your own ride, you'll need to rent a bike. No worries. Bicycle shops around the city rent and sell a staggering variety of types and brands. Shops are helpfully clustered near Golden Gate Park, for park and city riding, and Fisherman's Wharf, for waterfront excursions. The latter include the city's most popular ride, the mildly challenging nine-mile trek from the wharf across the Golden Gate Bridge and downhill into Sausalito, past the north end of the bridge.

Near Golden Gate Park, my favorite bike shop is **Avenue Cyclery** (756 Stanyan St., 387-3155). I bought a bike there and was impressed by the staff: they're knowledgeable without being overbearing (unlike their colleagues at some S.F. bike shops, where spoke-wheeled one-upmanship and attitude rule). If you're riding in the park, try John F. Kennedy Drive, a long east-west artery that winds past many of the park's prime attractions. Try to hit it on a Sunday, when the street is closed to cars. Just west of the park is another great ride, north and south along the eastern side of the Great Highway. The easy scenic route takes you past beachfront apartments and restored sand dunes close to the ocean.

At Fisherman's Wharf, check out **Blazing Saddles** near the Powell/ Mason cable car turnaround (1095 Columbus Ave., 202-8888) and at Pier 41. It, too, has a smart staff and a good selection, plus an innovative computer screen called a Computrak — a map with written directions to keep you from getting lost — that attaches to the handlebars.

The trip across the Golden Gate Bridge is breathtaking. Many people ride to Sausalito, and then take a Golden Gate ferry back to San Francisco to get out on the water. Biking on the S.F. side, you'll pass a circular building known to previous generations of San Franciscans as the Round House restaurant; now it's a souvenir shop. If you pedal across the Golden Gate Bridge, take the path on the west side, since the one on the east side is reserved for pedestrians. Some cyclists fail to get with the program, endangering seniors, disabled people, kids, and other walkers and runners, while simply slowing themselves down. Don't be one of them.

San Francisco has a frisky, occasionally ornery, bicycle culture, which plays out in interesting ways. Bike messengers hang out at **Harvey's Place** (330 Fifth St., 495-0448), a combination lunch counter, five-and-dime, grocery, and liquor store. The burgers and packaged junk food are cheap, the ambience is funky, and there is a mural done in the Japanese manga style on the outside wall. Harvey's has a liberal check-cashing service for regulars. Bike messengers also swarm along the concrete wall outside the round building at Sansome and Market streets.

The bicycle culture turns political during **Critical Mass**, when cyclists take to the streets en masse to make the point that bicycles are serious vehicles, not just toys. Critical Mass, which often infuriates motorists by putting hundreds of closely bunched riders on thoroughfares, started in San Francisco and spread to other cities around the globe. It is typically held the last Friday of every month, starting at 6 p.m. from Justin Herman Plaza at the foot of Market Street. There is no central planning or designated route. Just show up and see what happens. Or call the **S.F. Bicycle Coalition** (431-2453).

Bike boosters should also check out the **Duboce bicycle mural** (Duboce between Market and Church). It's on the back of the Safeway supermarket on a fairly grubby alley next to the streetcar line. A Critical Mass rider, artist Mona Caron, created the environmentally themed block-long painting. I once saw a drug deal go down there. The dealer — I swear I'm not making this up — sped off on a bicycle.

S E C R E T
BLUES

Chicago it ain't, nor is San Francisco the Mississippi delta. Nevertheless, San Franciscans love the enduring quality and rich emotional
coloration of the blues. Local talent and touring players plug in at
headliner clubs and down-and-dirty corner bars. And, once a year, the
city does a hot bump-and-grind at the San Francisco Blues Festival.

The premier blues club, owned by octogenarian blues legend John Lee
Hooker, is the **Boom Boom Room** (1601 Fillmore St., 673-8000).
Hooker, who lives in the Bay Area, shows up occasionally at the club.
It's located in the heart of the Fillmore district, which was once the
city's nerve center for blues and, especially, jazz. Appropriately dark
and noisy (there is live music and dancing five nights a week), and
often crowded, the Boom Boom Room is a venue for touring and
local pros.

Biscuits & Blues (401 Mason St., 292-2583) occupies a second-story
corner spot in a busy downtown location. The club, the local branch
of a national chain, has a full bar and a restaurant featuring decent
Southern cooking — thus, the biscuit part of the name. John Lee
Hooker's musician sons and daughter have crossed town to play Biscuits & Blues, and the venue books touring acts like Bobby Rush.

Several local bars are reliable places to hear blues by working-stiff
musicians. **Blue Lamp** (561 Geary St., 885-1464) is a no-nonsense
corner bar in the rough and ready Tenderloin. Electric Sundays and
acoustic Mondays are on the bill at this small neighborhood joint. In
North Beach, blues bands play seven nights a week at **The Saloon**
(1232 Grant Ave., 989-7666). The musicians are apt to be playing after

clocking out from their day jobs, and the crowd is older and boozy. The Saloon, pouring beer in the same wooden Victorian building since 1861, claims to be S.F.'s oldest bar; some of its customers have apparently been drinking there since it opened. This is a place where you'll hear men talking in raspy, steel-wool voices. It's not an act; these folks are living the blues. **Powell's Place** (511 Hayes St., 863-1404) is a soul-food restaurant with a rockin' jukebox. There's blues and smooth soul on the box, and buttery cornmeal muffins on the menu.

Since starting in the 1970s, the **San Francisco Blues Festival** (979-5588 or www.sfblues.com) has grown in stature and size. It takes over the Great Meadow at Fort Mason, a bayside military-base-turned-arts center, for a weekend bash every fall. Producer/founder Tom Mazzolini is hard working and dedicated, and the festival has presented the likes of Willie Dixon, Big Mama Thornton, Elvin Bishop, Koko Taylor, and many others. This is a high-quality, high-spirited event.

SECRET
BRITISH

Oh, to be in England (or Scotland or Wales) now that you are here. Should you pine for the Auld Sod, there's no better place to hoist a pint of the real stuff than **Edinburgh Castle** (950 Geary St., 885-4074). A long, narrow pub on two levels — a central staircase leads to the mezzanine, with its red felt pool table and cozy booths — Edinburgh Castle pours imports, such as Boddington's, McEwan's

Export Ale, Strongbow hard cider, Guinness stout, and many others from the United Kingdom and Ireland. Indeed, this is an Irish-friendly Anglophile pub, with stacks of the free monthly *Irish Herald* newspaper and notices touting Celtic poets and rockers, as well as leaflets for lefty political causes. There is a winningly wide selection of Scotch whisky at the bar, and crispy fish 'n' chips are served in a classic newspaper wrap.

Fans of British football have their redoubt in the lower Haight at another pub, **Mad Dog in the Fog** (530 Haight St., 626-7279). Physically unprepossessing but welcoming, the Mad Dog has two dartboards, sells Brit food faves, such as bangers and mash, shepherd's pie, and beans on toast, and pours dozens of imports, including the fine London Pride. There's always football (that is, soccer) on the TV mounted above the bar, and British club shirts, banners, and other football memorabilia brighten the premises.

If tea is more to your taste, repair to the **Windsor Tea Room** of the **King George Hotel** (334 Mason St., 781-5050). The buttery tarts, the little white bread sandwiches with the crusts removed, the jam, the butter, the sugar, and, of course, the selection of English Breakfast, Earl Grey, and other teas, are all there in this modest theater district hotel with the Union Jack flag outside. For a ritzy afternoon tea, it would be very hard to beat the lobby lounge of the **Ritz-Carlton Hotel** (600 Stockton St., 296-7465). Although the Ritz-Carlton is not of British provenance, it serves a proper British-style tea. No less a personage than Chris Patton, the last British governor of Hong Kong, told me it was the best tea he had had in America when I interviewed him in the lounge. Even in England, the tea lover distressingly often finds teas made with teabags. Not at the Ritz-Carlton, where loose teas are used for a brew that is fresh and flavorful.

Anglophile shoppers are not without recourse. **N. Peal** (80 Grant Ave., 421-2713), sells men's and women's clothing from its downtown shop, and has fine Scottish cashmere goods on offer. **Thomas Pink** (255 Post St., 421-2022), the upmarket men's wear shop in London's tiny, tony Jermyn Street, maintains a sizable branch just off Union Square, where it stocks Egyptian-cotton shirts and other fine attire. It only rains in San Francisco in winter, but should you find yourself drenched, **Burberry** (225 Post St., 392-2200) would undoubtedly enjoy the opportunity to keep you dry in style. If your tastes are Scottish, check out **Hector Russell Scottish Imports** (76 Geary St., 989-5458). Russell sells single-malt Scottish whiskies, Scottish kitsch (key chains bearing the name of clans), corny bumper stickers (sample: "Bagpipe Spoken Here"), tartans, kilts, and other goods from north of Hadrian's Wall.

SECRET
BURMESE

Burma — known by the post-colonial name Myanmar since 1989 — calls itself the Golden Land, but it's very much the Unknown Land to North Americans. More's the pity, because it is a fascinating country, rich in culture and history, though plagued by violent, fractious politics. I went there in the spring of 2000 and was enchanted by the place. Since then, like many a returned traveler, I have been trying to recapture the experience, as much as I can, in my hometown.

The Burmese community in San Francisco is smaller and more low key than most immigrant communities from Pacific Rim countries, but a cluster of restaurants and a church offer tastes of the cuisine and culture of this remote Asian land.

The **First Burmese Baptist Church** (380 21st Ave., 751-3834) is something of a novelty, since most people in Burma — oops, Myanmar — are Buddhists (with a sprinkling of Hindus). Nevertheless, there it is, conducting bilingual services. The church occupies an old building that has been modified with discreet Asian architectural touches, in the foggy precincts of the cool, breezy Richmond district — a locale that differs sharply from hot, tropical Myanmar.

If food for the body appeals more than food for the soul, half a dozen Burmese restaurants have opened in recent years. They generally set up shop in Chinese neighborhoods and offer half Burmese, half Chinese menus. Two places stand out, and they are cheap — a novelty in this expensive city.

Irrawaddy Burmese Cuisine (1769 Lombard St., 931-2830) is the most upscale Burmese eatery in the city. Even so, Irrawaddy — named for the country's major river — is reasonably priced and savory. "Dainty eggplant" is cooked in onions, tomatoes, paprika, and dried shrimp powder in tamarind sauce. Burmese beef curry shows the influence of India, Myanmar's western neighbor. Mohingar is a bracing fish soup. Service is relaxed but attentive. Irrawaddy, somewhat tucked away on roaring Lombard Street, is often uncrowded.

Mandalay (4348 California St., 386-3895) is slightly cheaper, and even better. It serves an exquisite ginger salad bursting with flavor. The server mixes it at your table, explaining what everything is: ginger thread, lentil seed, coconut chips, peanuts, and a subtly spiced dressing. Mandalay eggplant combines eggplant with lemongrass, tomato sauce, and ground shrimp to palate-pleasing effect. A cooling shredded coconut and tapioca drink is chewy and sweet, and comes with a spoon and large plastic straw for vacuuming up the tapioca pearls at the bottom of the glass. Mandalay is also health-minded enough to prepare anything on the menu without salt if you tell the server first.

These two unpretentious, inexpensive restaurants could put many a pricier, haughtier restaurant to shame.

Myanmar — oh, heck, Burma — is also home to skilled silversmiths, goldsmiths, and makers of lovely lacquer ware and marionettes. Imported crafts from Burmese artisans are not easy to find, but **Asia Galleries** (1538 Grant Ave., 392-9127) stocks fine work from Burma, as well as other still-exotic Southeast Asian countries: Laos, Nepal, and Cambodia.

SECRET
CABLE CARS

Of course, you know about the famous cable cars, which rival the Golden Gate Bridge as icons of San Francisco. Every year, 10 million people ride the cable cars. (They're not streetcars or trolleys, as they run on underground metal cables and don't have engines.) What most of the millions don't know is that you don't have to line up at the scuzzy cable car turnarounds at Powell and Market or Fisherman's Wharf, where you'll be besieged by shirtless buskers, street preachers, and spare change artists for up to an hour. No. You can board anywhere on any of the three lines anytime the cars stop, which they do frequently. The conductor will be happy to take your two bucks. Another thing: the lines are shorter at Market and California streets, outside the Hyatt Regency Hotel, and almost non-existent at California Street and Van Ness Avenue — other places where the cable cars come to the end of the line and turn around. When you ride, stand on the running boards outside; don't even think about the claustrophobic

interiors of these small, antique conveyances. The views are much
better outside, and you'll pass close enough to people on the cable
cars going in the other direction to high-five them.

SECRET
CHURCHES

San Francisco has scads of churches, along with temples, synagogues,
mosques, and other places of worship. The most well-known Christian churches are famous for being big or for playing a significant
social role. For example, **Grace Cathedral Episcopal Church**, high
atop Nob Hill, is known for its High Church seriousness and *Social
Register* congregation. **Glide Memorial United Methodist Church**,
in the gritty Tenderloin, is known for its ebullient, musical "Sunday
celebrations," its liberal activist ministry, and its media connections
(and, thus, media visibility). The most interesting churches for the
visitor are smaller places, often located outside the city center.

My shortlist of great churches begins with the smallest and arguably
most beautiful: the **Swedenborgian Church** (2107 Lyon St., 346-
6466) in leafy, tony Presidio Heights. The church's namesake,
Emanuel Swedenborg (1688-1772), was a Christian mystic who influ-
enced the American Transcendentalists, as well as the great Irish poet
W.B. Yeats, and the Argentine novelist and short-story master Jorge
Luis Borges. The main building, which dates from 1895, is easy to
miss behind its textured gray concrete wall. The street entrance is
under a small, understated portico.

A compact jewel of a garden borders the Swedenborgian Church on the south side. Inside the church, the wood-vaulted nave shelters sturdy wooden chairs with seats of woven rushes; they have something of the plain elegance of Shaker furniture. A working fireplace at one end of the nearly square nave is flanked by stacked firewood and topped with pinecones, while stained-glass windows overlook the garden. Major figures from the Bay Region architectural movement at the turn of the 20th century, including A. Page Brown and Bernard Maybeck, designed various parts of the church complex. Their gifts are much in evidence in this serene place, a hymn to silence.

A century older, dating to 1791, is **Mission Dolores** (16th and Dolores, 621-8203), the oldest building in the city. Spanish Franciscans founded it as one link in a chain of Roman Catholic churches from San Diego to Sonoma, north of San Francisco. The original basilica has four-foot-thick adobe walls and a hushed air of antiquity. The parish church next to the basilica is still used regularly for services. Also inside the mission complex is a small museum that gives visitors a glimpse into the early life of San Francisco. Indeed, the mission's formal name, Mision San Francisco de Asis, gave the city its name.

Behind the church is a small cemetery, hushed and historic. Hispanic and Yankee pioneers are buried there, amid meticulously tended roses — red, yellow, white, pink — plus rosemary, nasturtiums, and poplars. "In memory of Sarah Rollins, who departed this life Sept. 9, A.D. 1851, aged 22 years old, and her infant son, R.E. Rollins," reads one tombstone. "Aqui reposa los resto mortales de Dona Francisca Granados, natural de Sonora, Mejico," reads another.

For something completely different, pay a visit to the **African Orthodox Church of St. John Coltrane**. First, you'll have to track down the church through its Web site: www.saintjohncoltrane.org.

The Divisadero Street storefront where the church's jazz services were formerly held is shuttered, and the congregation is moving around.

Inspired by the cosmic music of Coltrane, the giant of exploratory jazz saxophone who died in 1967, pastor Franzo Wayne King blows his own soprano sax and other musicians join in before the sermons. In the old Divisadero place, the walls were covered with artwork exalting Coltrane, and the church became a favorite of local white hipsters. However, the mostly African American parishioners don't put air quotes around anything, and if you listen to their founding document, Coltrane's album *A Love Supreme*, you'll know why. No smirking irony. Just purity and passion.

SECRET
CINEMA

The movies love San Francisco, and San Francisco loves the movies.

Since the early days of cinema, when the 1903 ur-feature *The Great Train Robbery* was shot in nearby Niles Canyon, San Francisco and its environs have been crawling with movie stars, directors, and their entourages. The city itself has become a screen character, starring in movies such as Erich von Stroheim's *Greed*, Humphrey Bogart's *The Maltese Falcon*, Clint Eastwood's Dirty Harry law 'n' order fantasies, Alfred Hitchcock's *Vertigo*, Phil Kaufman's shrewdly creepy 1978 remake of *Invasion of the Body Snatchers*, and *Groove*, a 2000 feature about the Ecstasy-fueled rave scene. The most thrilling of all movie car chases, the centerpiece of Steve McQueen's S.F. cop flick *Bullitt*, is often imitated, never duplicated. Of course, you've seen the city in

Festival, produced by the S.F.-based distribution company Frameline, is held every June, coinciding with the huge Pride march. The **San Francisco Jewish Film Festival**, founded in 1981 and held in summer, is the world's oldest Jewish film fest. It screens a particularly fine selection of European imports. The **Asian American International Film Festival** is a strong vehicle for works from or about Asian Pacific cultures. Small independent and art films are showcased every November in the **Film Arts Film Festival**, and once or twice a month at the Yerba Buena Center for the Arts (Third and Mission, 978-2787), where the **San Francisco Cinematheque**, a thoughtful champion of personal filmmaking since 1961, screens shorts, experimental work, and documentaries in a state-of-the-art setting.

A few movie stars live in the city, among them Sharon Stone, Robin Williams, Danny Glover, and Joan Chen. The most accessible star is the community-minded Williams, who is seen on the streets of San Francisco more often than he is seen in good movies.

There are a few other things you should know. **Landmark Theater Corporation**, a national chain of art houses founded with a single-screen house in Berkeley, has five cinemas in S.F., and sells discount cards good for 10 feature films at any Landmark theater. Landmark's **Bridge Theatre** (3010 Geary Blvd., 751-3212) and **Clay Theatre** (2261 Fillmore St., 352-0810) are delightful single-screen neighborhood houses.

This is a book about San Francisco, not the Bay Area as a whole, but I would be remiss if I didn't tell you about two other venues worth a drive out of town. One is the **Pacific Film Archive** (2575 Bancroft Way, Berkeley, 510-642-1412), a superb cinema that screens two different movies every day. It's educational in the best sense. You cross San Francisco Bay to get there. The other is the **Rafael Film Center** (1118 Fourth St., San Rafael, 454-1222), a non-profit cinema ensconced in a beautiful Art Deco theater restored in 1999 and programmed by the producers of the annual Mill Valley Film Festival. The Rafael has three plush auditoriums and shows an intelligent mix of new releases, revivals, kids' stuff, and foreign and independent work. You cross the Golden Gate Bridge to Marin County to get there.

Finally, lest we forget: the best movie theater coffee is at the Roxie. And the best movie theater popcorn is in the Landmark cinemas, the Castro, and the Rafael. They all pop it fresh, they don't reuse semi-rancid oil, and they use real butter, not the odiferous, soy-based stuff that can knock a person down at 20 paces.

SECRET
CLASSICAL

At the top of the artistic food chain are the Big Three: the **San Francisco Opera** (864-3330), a world-class company that stages its productions in the War Memorial Opera House, a beautiful 1932 building splendidly restored in 1997; the **San Francisco Symphony** (864-6000), led by the charismatic Michael Tilson Thomas, which plays at modern Louise M. Davies Symphony Hall; and the **San Francisco Ballet** (865-2000), founded in 1932 and America's oldest professional ballet company, which dances in the War Memorial Opera House. All of these first-rate companies are worthy of your attention, but all get massive exposure, so we'll speak no more of them here.

It is entirely possible to catch professional classical music for free, or nearly free, at a number of city churches. Not only is the price right,

the venues are intimate and classy without being intimidating. There are fine classical concerts at **Old St. Mary's Cathedral** (660 California St., 288-3800), built in 1854; **Old First Presbyterian Church** (1751 Sacramento St., 474-1608); **First Unitarian Universalist Church** (1187 Franklin St., 776-4580); and **St. Patrick's Church** (756 Mission St., 777-3211). **St. Mary's Cathedral**, a huge modern structure opened in 1970 (1111 Gough St., 567-3775), specializes in organ concerts.

Also noteworthy (though not free): the worthy **San Francisco Performances** (392-4400) presents classical, jazz, and other concerts; **Pocket Opera** (575-1100) produces scaled-down versions of classic operas, some running just an hour, at affordable prices; the **Women's Philharmonic** (437-0123), which specializes in premieres and revivals of works by female composers and is led by female conductors, bills itself as the only women's classical orchestra in the United States; and **San Francisco Camerata Americana** (587-2319 or www.sfcamerata.org) is the only professional orchestra in the United States that devotes itself entirely to performing music of Latin America and work by Latin American composers.

The city's de facto Culture Gulch is an area of several square blocks west of City Hall, where the Opera House, Herbst Theatre, Davies Symphony Hall, and San Francisco Ballet school and business office are concentrated, along with a profusion of art galleries, restaurants, cafes, and shops. Even the parking garage has an arty identity: it's called the Performing Arts Garage. An upscale neighborhood hotel, the **Inn at the Opera** (333 Fulton St., 863-8400), hosts touring musicians. I attended a post-concert dinner for the Canadian guitarist Liona Boyd there and was charmed by the hotel's intimate, European feel.

Several blocks from the Inn at the Opera is another cosy, well-kept hotel with a classical connection. The **Abigail Hotel** (246 McAllister

St., 398-0400) provides a home away from home for visiting musicians playing classical sounds; the Abigail is also the home of **Millennium** (487-9800), one of the city's premier vegetarian restaurants. As you walk around the Civic Center area, you're apt to bump into denizens of Culture Gulch; the angular beauty sipping tea or designer water at **Parco Coffee & Tea** (350 Hayes St., 621-1348) is probably a dancer. Not in the neighborhood, but worth the short trip, is **Byron Hoyt** (2525 16th St., 431-8055), another great shop, where you can buy recordings and published scores. Careful you don't miss it; it's up on the top floor. The Classical Annex at **Tower Records** (2568 Jones St., 441-4880) has an extensive stock of recordings. Not inclined to spend the money or the time shopping for recordings? Listen to the classics on radio station KDFC (102.1 FM), the city's all-classical station, and check out upcoming classical music events on the station's Web site, www.kdfc.com.

If you love opera, you'll be entertained in North Beach. On Saturday afternoons at 2 p.m., **Caffe Trieste** (601 Vallejo St., 392-6739) features members of the Giotta family, who own the place, singing operatic arias and popular American songs, accompanied by piano and accordion. Get there by 1:30 if you want a table, though you can hear fine from the sidewalk. There's no charge for the music, and the Trieste's espresso is as good as any in town. **Tosca Cafe** (242 Columbus Ave., 986-9651) has beautiful operatic pieces on the jukebox, along with Sinatra and other cool song stylists. Oh, one more thing: if you go to the S.F. Opera, the back of the first balcony has especially good acoustics.

SECRET

COCKTAILS

If you go out for cocktails, you'll notice one thing right away — most of the places pouring sky-blue and blood-red liquids into Y-shaped glasses are strangely lacking in blue air: there's no tobacco smoke. Since January 1, 1998, it's been illegal to smoke indoors in California workplaces, even bars. The idea is to eliminate second-hand smoke. Some bar owners and patrons complain bitterly, and some flout the law, but businesses risk a hefty fine for doing so — so most comply.

Without a cigarette in your hand or pouting mouth, it really is a challenge to approximate the ring-a-ding-ding retro style of Sinatra and the Rat Pack. Yet, many of the city's twentysomethings (and a few of their elders) manage. And they get a lot of help from alcohol at places where finer forms of booze are served. Here is an even dozen cocktail connections. I like 'em because they pour great drinks, because they're great places to drink, or both.

Bix (56 Gold Alley, 433-6300) is your way upmarket place for classy drinking. It's located in a swank former gold assay office on an old brick-lined alley. In fact, the building is on the National Register of Historic Places. Bix is a two-level bar and restaurant with a sweeping staircase leading to intimate tables on the mezzanine. The sweet Bix Punch is a popular order here. I fancy Bix's big martini, straight up with a twist, made with Belvedere vodka.

Just a short, lurching walk from Bix is the **Bubble Lounge** (714 Montgomery St., 434-4204), another classy place. The Bubble Lounge is the sibling of its namesake in New York, and serves 300 brands of champagne, 20 of them by the glass; that's where the bubbles come from. Outside the back door on Hotaling Street, a one-block alley, you'll see metal poles topped by metal horses' heads. You're not hallucinating; they resemble hitching posts from Wild West days. It is amazing, is it not, to know that the West is actually east of San Francisco? Have another glass of champagne.

While on the upmarket end, don't miss the aptly named **Grand Cafe** in the **Hotel Monaco** (501 Geary St., 292-0101), which excels at things cocktail, and serves superior food in an almost Art Nouveau environment that some have likened to a Paris train station. It's absolutely gorgeous. This is a good place to nurse your drink and make it last.

For millennium style — and a generous hand with the cosmopolitans — you can't beat the bar at the **W Hotel** (181 Third St., 817-7836). When it opened in 1999, the W quickly became the hottest source of cool in town, and it still is. The first time I went to the bar there, I was dressed in black. Mistake. The hotel employees dress in black. I thought guests were going to ask me to show them to their room. Given that this hotel and bar draw maybe the best-looking, most affluent clientele in the city, that might not have been so bad. Get there by 7 p.m.

They march to a different drummer in the Mission district; they even imbibe to a different drummer. At the salon-meets-saloon **Beauty Bar** (2299 Mission St., 285-0323), the mostly female clientele sips cocktails — cosmopolitans are favored — while their nails are buffed. A great place in the Mission hipster zone is **Luna Park** (694 Valencia St., 553-8584). It serves very good new American food, with savory items, such as chèvre fondue and ricotta-filled ravioli with roasted eggplant. With just 49 seats, the place quickly fills up, with noise bouncing off the hard surfaces and reaching painful levels. But a well-chosen wine list and superb cocktails make it a prime place to drink. The mojitos with fresh leaves of mint are super.

North Beach, always a fun neighborhood, is loaded with cocktail lounges. The **Hi-Ball Lounge** (473 Broadway, 39-SWING) is a dark, Vegas-baby! hangout for swing kids. The name says it all. A few feet up the hill, secreted in the **Basque Hotel** (15 Romolo Place, 398-1359), is **15 Romolo**. This bar is hard to describe if only because it is so dark that it's hard to see. Suffice it to say, it is a hipster bar, small but generous when pouring cocktails.

A block south, a very different scene unfolds at **Tosca Cafe** (242 Columbus Ave., 986-9651). Young and older drinkers mix with uncommon ease in a place with warm-toned images of Italy on the walls, opera and Sinatra on the juke, and a VIP room in the back you won't get into unless you're with Nic Cage, Sean Penn, or club-hopping Mayor Willie Brown. Try the house "cappuccino": hot chocolate, sugar, and brandy. It's delicious.

There's more swing dancing and styling going on at **Club Deluxe** (1511 Haight St., 552-6949), which some cultural pundits credit with starting the swing craze. Scorpions, cosmos, and other cocktails fuel the activity. For something different, and better than it sounds, try the "saketails" at any of the three ZAO **Noodle Bars** around town. Although I still prefer sake as it's served in Japan — chilled, to bring out the flavor, and not mixed — ZAO has come up with something. The ginger-tini will, if nothing else, wake you up. It's sake shaken over ice with ginger juice and pickled ginger garnish.

For your full-strength cocktail needs, I recommend **Lisa's on Folsom** (299 Ninth St., 551-1688). Lisa's is a nouveau Asian restaurant that makes a super spiced noodle soup, among other things, but what it's really good at making is vodka infusions with drunken fruit. The vodka-marinated fruit sits in big glass jars in the window for who knows how long before it's plopped into your glass. When you get to the fruit at the bottom of your 10-ounce glass, you will know alcohol. And Lisa's is open till 4 a.m. on weekends.

Get the designated driver NOW, and buckle up.

S E C R E T
C O F F E E

The Starbucks death star hasn't obliterated everything in sight, at least not yet. Indeed, San Francisco is doubly blessed when it comes to coffee. It has a strong Italian flavor in North Beach, the core of the city's traditional coffee culture, as well as an encouragingly large number of quirky neighborhood cafes and coffeehouses that continue to flourish in the age of franchising.

My vote for best espresso-based Italian coffee is split between Caffe Trieste and Caffe Roma, both in North Beach and absolutely dependable. Significantly, both caffes — they use the Italian spelling — roast their beans on the premises.

Caffe Trieste (601 Vallejo St., 392-6739) has the edge in atmosphere. It's an old beatnik hangout, with framed vintage photos mounted on the wall, a few tables on the sidewalk outside, and a free Saturday afternoon musicale (see Secret Classical). You can't miss with the espresso drinks, and the pastries and snacks are good. **Caffe Roma** (526 Columbus Ave., 296-7942) is another caffeinated Old Faithful. The fresh-roasted beans smell and taste terrific, and the espresso drinks and light foods in this sparkling space are first rate. Check out the big brass roasting machine in the window.

If Roma and Trieste are too crowded, head up Grant Avenue to the **North End Caffe** (1402 Grant Ave., 956-3350), a hole-in-the-wall place with a cozy upstairs alcove and generous double espressos that nearly overflow the cup. If you're walking around North Beach, which is the best way to get around, you'll probably also smell the aroma from **Graffeo Coffee Roasting Company**, which sells beans to many of the neighborhood restaurants. If you want a scrumptious pick-me-up, order an affogato at **Caffe Greco** (423 Columbus Ave., 397-6261); affogato is a shot of espresso over gelato.

The best chain coffee in town, by far, is at **Peet's Coffee & Tea**. Started as a single store in Berkeley in 1966 by Dutch-born, Indonesia-raised Alfred Peet, the business now has nine San Francisco locations (800-999-2132). Peet's coffees are much stronger than most North Americans are used to, without the acidic edge of truck-stop swill. Peet's is also a good place to buy yummy snacks like chocolate-covered coffee beans and coffee accessories. The very best place for coffee-makers, however, is **Thomas E. Cara** (517 Pacific Ave., 781-0383), which sells beautifully polished espresso machines, and nothing but — as large or small as you want, in a wide range of prices.

In the neighborhoods, every San Franciscan has a local for chattering, sipping, writing, reading, and hanging out. My picks begin with **Blue Danube** (306 Clement St., 387-8025), a place filled with character (and sometimes characters) tucked away in the inner Richmond. Every tabletop has an original design and original artwork adorns the walls. There are big windows that open onto the street, a few sidewalk tables, and a PC or two for logging onto the Internet. On top of all this, the coffee is good, and the hip young staff is friendly. Another good place on Clement is **Java Source** (343 Clement St., 387-8025), which has a big back room overflowing with free newspapers and handbills, and an even bigger front room that's open to the street scene.

If you're downtown and dying to check your e-mail while you knock back a latte, go to **Seven** (701 Mission St., 243-0930), the cafe at the Yerba Buena Center for the Arts. Seven has decent java and a great selection of local, national, and international zines. You'll recognize it by the line of candy gumdrop-flavored — er, colored — iMacs in the window. The only drawback is that Seven doesn't stay open late.

Finally, if you're dying to get away from the congestion and electron-like commotion of downtown, go to Potrero Hill, a quietly hip neighborhood near downtown but just far enough away. Have a mocha java and meet the locals at **Thinkers Cafe** (1631 20th St., 285-8294), which serves up full-flavored joe. Get the establishment's Frequent Thinkers card; if you go back, the 11th cup of coffee is free with your card — making you a freethinker, of course.

SECRET
COMEDY

Long ago, in a galaxy far, far away — actually, the 1980s in San Francisco — I was the comedy critic for the *San Francisco Examiner*. My mission: to find the next Robin Williams or Whoopi Goldberg, superstars who had just emerged from the Bay Area comedy club scene (Williams) and experimental theater scene (Goldberg), and to crown the new king or queen of comedy in the smudgy pages of the newspaper. As it turned out, there was no new local superstar of that magnitude waiting in the wings.

Since then, the scene has atrophied in size, though not necessarily in talent, going from four full-time comedy clubs in the 1980s to two today. They are the **Punchline** (444 Battery St., 397-7573), a local branch of a national chain, located in the Embarcadero Center downtown, and **Cobb's** (2801 Leavenworth St., 928-4320), on the northern waterfront in The Cannery — once the world's largest peach cannery, now thoroughly renovated. The Punchline features touring national acts and is professionally run, but I prefer Cobb's, which mixes national headliners with up-and-coming local talent, and is locally owned and managed by Tom Sawyer. Yes, that's a real guy named Tom Sawyer, not a Mark Twain character. Cobb's and the Punchline have the usual cover charges at the door and two-drink minimums.

For cutting-edge comedy and satire in funkier environs, check out the **Mock Cafe** at **The Marsh** (1062 Valencia St., 826-5750), in the heart of the arty hipster zone in the Mission district. The Marsh, a great place for alternative theater, poetry, and performance art, presents a comedy showcase Saturday nights. Robin Williams has been known to show up and do a set just to keep his hand in. No telling whether you'll see him, and no telling what he'll do; he likes to wing it. More predictably, you can catch regular weekend shows of **Bay Area Theatresports** (Fort Mason Center, Building B, third floor, 474-8935). Local theater and comedy pros do improvisation based on audience suggestions. They're on if you are. Theatresports has a rule against gratuitous racist and sexist humor. That may sound stuffy, but as a reviewer who endured endless woman baiting by insecure male comics, pathetic dick jokes, and lowlife language by stand-ups who should've sat down, I can assure you it makes sense.

The big bashes in Bay Area comedy include **Comedy Day**, started in the 1980s by local stand-up Jose Simon and held in late summer at the Polo Field in Golden Gate Park (watch local listings and Web sites). It's an all-day affair, and it's free. The other big deal is the **San Francisco Comedy Competition** (again, check local listings), held in stages in various venues and ending in late summer. The work is of highly variable quality, but comedians vying for prize money and TV contracts give it all they've got and sometimes something extraordinarily funny happens.

SECRET
COMIX AND
CARTOONS

In the dear, not quite dead 1960s, San Francisco, along with New York, became the center of underground comix. Taboo-breaking strips and comic books mushroomed with the counterculture in the Haight-Ashbury and the Lower East Side. These comix-with-a-X produced gifted writer/artists like Robert (*Mr. Natural, Felix the Cat*) Crumb, Art Spiegelman (who won a Pulitzer Prize for his dark comic-novel *Maus*), and Bill Griffith, who put his *Zippy the Pinhead* into daily newspaper syndication. The comix underground helped make the comics form more fluid and its content more adult. Together with underground newspapers, comix gave rise to the feisty photocopy and Web site zine culture of today.

Comics and comix are still plentiful in San Francisco. In fact, there's an interesting shop using that name: **Comics & Comix** (650 Irving St., 665-5888), which carries a large assortment of published comic art, from mainstream to alternative. **Comix Experience** (305 Divisadero St., 863-9258) takes it further, retailing more edgy, extreme work in its storefront in the boho ghetto of the Western Addition neighborhood. Superhero stuff and other fare can be found at **Comic Outpost II** (2381 Ocean Ave., 239-2669). **Al's Comics, Cards & Toys** (491 Guerrero St., 861-1220) has a good selection and good ambience: comics in plastic covers on the wall and all over the shop, in cardboard cartons. **Cards & Comics Central** (5522 Geary Blvd., 668-3544) is another place to go for superhero games, miniatures, dolls, and other artifacts based on cartoon series, like the *South Park* characters. All these shops have the slightly musty, oddly satisfying smell of places with a lot of newsprint on hand, and are fine places for browsing. **Last Gasp** (777 Florida St., 824-6636), a long-time leader in distribution and comix publishing — it published the once-famous Zap! Comix — is run by founder/owner Ron Turner, the knowledgeable and dedicated Big Daddy of comix in the U.S. of A.

Cartoon art, which includes animated cartoons and daily newspaper panels, is showcased in the **Cartoon Art Museum** (814 Mission St., CAR-TOON). A non-profit institution dating from 1984, the museum is not as well known as it should be. It occupies the second floor of a building on a smelly downtown block above a liquor store and several other businesses. The Cartoon Art Museum won't impress you from the street, but it's engaging and ambitious inside, with 6,000 square feet of exhibition space, a kids' room, a bookstore, a research library, and impressive collections of original art. You can view pencil and line drawings by the likes of Garry Trudeau, Matt Groening, Charles Schulz of *Peanuts* fame, and the great Walt Kelley, creator of *Pogo*, on the wall and in display cases, as well as animated cartoons on TV monitors.

If you want toons with a cocktail, check out **POW** (278-0940), a young-hipster cocktail lounge on the corner of Sixth and Mission streets, in the enlarged purple heart of Skid Row. Japanese anime cartoons are deployed as decor inside, giving the bar a deliberately cartoonish flair. This corner used to be occupied by Poppy, on old-timers' dive where I'd see drinkers at the bar with longneck Buds at 9 a.m. as I walked past the open door on my way to work. POW's crowd is more likely to be calling it a night at 9 a.m. If you tire of the anime or decide there's not enough punch in the product for you, there's always the corner.

SECRET
COP BARS

You see the guy sitting in the corner with a cold one, pretending to scan the racing form? I happen to know he's a detective with the SFPD. And that woman at the end of the bar sipping her martini and looking over here when she thinks we don't notice? Homicide. She's with Homicide, I'm sure of it.

You could find yourself having these kind of thoughts in bars frequented by off-duty police officers when they go out "to debrief," in police parlance. Bars don't announce themselves as cop bars, and, indeed, police officers tend not to announce their presence, either, for security reasons. Back in the 1970s, a pipe bomb intended for a particular San Francisco Police Department officer exploded in the Line-Up, a now-defunct Seventh Street bar that was a hangout for off-duty cops. The bomb missed its intended target, but killed another customer.

Cop bars tend to be clustered near the SFPD's 10 neighborhood stations, with a diminishing number of debriefing parlors near the **Hall of Justice** (850 Bryant St.). Cop bars tend to be no-frills burger and beer places, or restaurant/bars where you can get a hearty meal and a drink. They're not glamorous but they have a certain gritty appeal. Once in a while, I used to drop into the Jay and Bee, a bar in the inner Mission that sported a collection of police badges from around the world. Sadly, it shut down a few years back.

In North Beach, near Central Station, **Capp's Corner** (1600 Powell St., 989-2589) is a family-friendly restaurant with bar that's been serving big, hearty, inexpensive meals, chiefly Italian food, for decades. It draws plenty of officers from the cop shop, as does **Gino & Carlo** (548 Green St., 421-0896), a dark, very local institution with a pool table. You'll feel like you're walking into a club or someone's home at Gino & Carlo, where you're likely to see patrons slamming down cups with dice on the bar. They're playing liar's dice to see who pays for the next round. Off-duty cops also stop in for a few at **North Star Cafe** (Vallejo and Powell, no listed phone), an unadorned neighborhood watering hole.

Down by the Hall of Justice, you can still see the faded signs of cop bars that have gone to the big holding pen in the sky, such as the Inn Justice and The Max. One place that is very much alive — and draws lawyers, too, by the looks of the crowd — is **Gin Joint** (312 Harriet St., 934-1655), located on an alley under Dad's Bail Bonds and a few feet from an unused rail spur. Befitting its name, Gin Joint has an impressive lineup of gin. It also sells craft beers like Full Sail, and vodka, such as locally made Skyy Vodka and velvety imported Belvedere. Like the rest of S.F., the Hall of Justice area is being gentrified. Directly across the street from the Hall is a branch of **Caffe Roma** (885 Bryant St., 431-8555), the excellent North Beach-based coffee roaster and maker of great espresso and java drinks. It's only open during the day, though.

Places that never close are the 24-hour bail bonds offices; there are 10 of them within a few yards of the Hall. If you walk down Bryant and peer through the big picture window into **Barrish Bail Bonds** (869 Bryant St.), see whether you can spot a guy with a corona of gray hair combed straight back. That's Jerry Barrish; when he's not bailing people out of jail, he's one of San Francisco's better playwrights.

SECRET
DANCE CLUBS

You got your house, you got your acid jazz, you got your hip-hop, your techno, your swing. Plenty of places for dancing fools to get down and get off, most with DJs, some with bands, all with powerful sound systems that'll cause your chest to cave in. They are so loud that there, like, won't be any need to, you know, converse. Many clubs are clustered South of Market, with some located downtown, in North Beach, and elsewhere. Here are some hot places favored by the locals.

DNA **Lounge** (375 11th St., 626-1409), a lavish dance club, has been going strong since the mid-'80s, which must be more than a century in dog years. DNA is still stylish, and stays open till 7 a.m. The hot new club of 2000, **Ruby Skye** (420 Mason St., 693-0777), is a huge, flashy place on three levels, where you can shoot pool, imbibe cocktails at the retro-futurist bar, and, of course, dance. Note that the club proclaims "appropriate fashionable attire required," meaning you won't get in if they don't like the way you're dressed. It's open till 4 a.m. Friday and Saturday. **Ten 15** (1015 Folsom St., 431-1200) has attitude at the door, acres of space for drinking and disco on five dance floors, and imported British DJs on Saturday nights. It stays open till 7 a.m. **Polly Esther's** (181 Eddy St., 885-1977) is a big, giddy Tenderloin club that reprises the sounds and styles of the '70s (upstairs) and '80s (downstairs), and features "Wonder Woman Thursday," when ladies are admitted free. Open till 4 a.m.

After the thumping, multilevel discos, the following clubs are smallish. But they're also stylish and have more personality than most. **Justice League** (628 Divisadero St., 289-2038) is a deliberately rough-hewn club that caters to the hip-hop and altie-rock crowd. It features DJs and live music, and spoken-word performances and poetry slams in addition to dancing. Wednesdays after work you can dance yourself into a trance with techno at "Qool" night at **111 Minna** (111 Minna St., 974-1719), an alternative art gallery when it's not hosting dancers; be advised, this midweek break ends about 9 p.m. Wednesdays are also "Dark Sparkle" night at **Cafe Du Nord** (2170 Market St., 861-5016), an underground club that is literally underground (i.e., downstairs). Dark Sparkle brings city Goths out to play and dance. For Latin dancing, **Roccapulco** (3140 Mission St., 648-6611) is a hot salsa spot in the outer Mission district.

What if you want to dance but don't know how? Wallflowers, rejoice. Potrero Hill's **Metronome Ballroom** (1830 17th St., 252-9000) is a neighborhood dance school during the week. On weekend nights, this big, handsome space morphs into an alcohol-free dance club.

SECRET

DIM SUM

You probably know the dim sum drill, but if not: dim sum consists of little Chinese snacks, often fried or steamed dumplings, the equivalent of tapas in Latin American cuisine. In some places, servers wheel food carts around and lift the lids on steaming containers to let you look at the food. You pick and pay, usually by the piece.

Here's a secret, known to San Franciscans, that visitors seem loath to believe: the best Chinese food is usually not found in Chinatown, at least not in the historic Chinatown near downtown. It's in the new, de facto Chinatowns on the west side of the city, in the Sunset and, especially, the Richmond along Geary Boulevard and Clement Street.

Canton and other areas of south China are the historical points of origin for most San Francisco Chinese Americans, so there are plenty of Cantonese restaurants. Dim sum is a standby of Cantonese cookery, although restaurants serving other Chinese regional food may have dim sum, too. The choices of where to dine on dim sum can be overwhelming, and every San Franciscan has a personal favorite or two. Here are mine.

Chinese American friends told me about the **R&G Lounge** (631 Kearny St., 982-7877), and it immediately became one of my faves. There's a banquet room upstairs, and hostesses wearing headsets, but informality reigns downstairs in a bright, clean, mirrored room. If you speak Chinese, or are with someone who does, you may well get better food; some of the most scrumptious items aren't on the English menu. Just smile and point if you see someone else eating something that looks good; that usually works. The R&G is known for its seafood.

Many non-dim sum entrees are great, too. I'm crazy about the prawns with honeyed walnuts, and the seasonal live crab with salt and pepper is outstanding.

Harbor Village (4 Embarcadero Center, 781-8833) is another place I was introduced to, independently, by executives from the Hong Kong Economic and Trade Office, and Tai Seng Video, a leading importer of Asian movies. They were both spot on. Incredibly good pork buns, little pancakes with scallions, spareribs — you name it, it's practically all good. The food is dished up by an efficient staff in a light-filled setting in the high-rise Embarcadero Center office and shopping complex.

Yank Sing has three downtown locations, is usually packed, and serves a mixed crowd of Asians and non-Asians, though some of my Chinese American friends find it too Americanized. Maybe, but there are some choice morsels on the menu.

An even better choice in the outer Richmond, a district usually unknown to tourists, is **Ton Kiang** (5821 Geary Blvd., 386-8530). Food is literally a matter of taste, of course, but there's probably not a truly bad dish in the house. Ton Kiang is sparkly and bright, yet somewhat nondescript. The energy goes into the food: shrimp-chive dumplings, foil-wrapped morsels of chicken, packages of sticky rice, all finished off with mango pudding.

Fans of Chinese cooking can't live by dim sum alone, to be sure. I am fond of Shanghai cuisine, provided it's not too heavy on the oil and salt. A great place for Shanghai food is **Fountain Court** (354 Clement St., 668-1100), another Richmond district redoubt. Noodles and braised fish stand out here, and the Shanghai Pot-au-feu — long-simmered broth with ham, pork ribs, bamboo shoots, and tofu, cooked in a clay pot — is delicious and nourishing. If you want food without MSG, salt, or oil, tell the staff first.

If you're up late, trolling the town, you'll want to stop into the absolutely no-frills, incredibly good **Yuet Lee** (1300 Stockton St., 982-6020). It's open till 3 a.m. and serves amazingly good catfish cooked with smoked pork, plus salt and pepper prawns and more. It's also very cheap, which is good, because Yuet Lee doesn't accept credit cards.

If you're up really late and have an uncontrollable craving for chicken's feet, you can find them south of the midnight hour at **Silver Restaurant** (737 Washington St., 433-8888), in old Chinatown. I had chicken's feet in Beijing, and found that their taste and texture is exactly what you'd expect, but these rubbery items are popular appetizers in China. You eat them — well, gnaw them — after dipping them in hot sauce.

S E C R E T
DISABLED ACCESS

Its fabled hills and historic landmark buildings can make San Francisco a daunting destination for disabled travelers, especially if they have limited mobility. Indeed, some famous tourist attractions are pretty inaccessible, notably the cable cars, which, as national historical monuments, can't be modified to accept wheelchairs.

That being said, the city is rolling out the welcome ramp to disabled travelers, especially now that their numbers are growing with the aging of the Baby Boomers. At times, progress is slow and achieved under pressure. It took a lawsuit to force the installation of an elevator at Hallidie Plaza, so that the disabled could avoid the steps down to the **Visitors Center** (foot of Market and Powell, 391-2000). Even after all that, the elevator is in effect a secret feature. It's often out of service.

But, things are getting better. Some **Municipal Railway** buses are equipped with front-door lifts to allow people in wheelchairs to board, there are curb cuts citywide, and newer buildings are usually accessible. My young niece Kelsey, who uses a wheelchair, was especially at ease in **Metreon** (101 Fourth St., 369-6000), the Sony Corp.'s entertainment center and retail complex, and **Zeum** (Fourth and Howard, 777-2800), a children's technology museum, both opened in 1999. Zeum incorporates a long, curving, central ramp as a key design element; it's both lovely and practical.

Until the late 1990s, the old federal penitentiary on **Alcatraz Island** (Blue & Gold Fleet reservation line, 705-5555) was, in effect, inaccessible to people with mobility problems. Now, the Rock and its steep terrain are traversed by free SEAT motorized vehicles that meet every second ferry calling at the island. Older folks and people who are just feeling poorly can use the vehicles, too.

The best single source of comprehensive information is the 32-page booklet *San Francisco Access 2000*, available free at the Visitors Center in Hallidie Plaza, with details on restaurants, hotels, museums, and other attractions. The chief contributor to the booklet, Berkeley activist Bonnie Lewkowicz, has a northern California-specific Web site at accessna.com. Some commercial travel outfits tailor information for disabled travelers; one of the best is Access-Able Travel Service (www.access-able.com, 303-232-2979). The Society for Advancement of Travel for the Handicapped (www.sath.org, 212-447-7284) is an authoritative national source of information about a variety of destinations and situations.

SECRET
DIVES

One person's dive is another person's refuge and cherished local. So just what constitutes a dive is subjective. But maybe we can agree that every bar we can even begin to think of as a dive has some features in common with the others: it is badly overdone, or baldly no-frills. It is cheap, which, of course, can be a redeeming factor and an important element in its appeal. It seems of another time, or in a time zone all its own. It can be dangerous, although the danger is more often to the visitor's psyche than the visitor's body.

Let us begin with the **Tee Off** (3129 Clement St., 752-5439). The Tee Off is, I believe, called that because it's across the street from the Lincoln Park Golf Course, not because its patrons are "teed-off," although they might be. The Tee Off has blues and country on the juke box, a pool room that seems more dive-like than the place as a whole, and sports on the bar TVs. Occasionally, drunken college boys celebrating a rite of passage at El Mansour, the belly-dancing emporium next door, wander in by mistake. The Tee Off is receptive to 'tude, tattoos, and tobacco. I left smelling like I had spent a whole week at an R.J. Reynolds company reunion, and I don't smoke.

Nearby, also in the outer Richmond, is **Trad'r Sam** (6150 Geary Blvd., 221-0773), a leading purveyor of tiki interior design and tropical drinks. A neighborhood watering hole by day, it's party central at night, a mix of slumming cocktail kids, and guys with motorcycles and Camaros who plan to party all night at the beach. When I was last there, an elderly lady told an elderly gent, "I couldn't find the car. I was drinkin' heavy then. I'm not drinkin' heavy now." Booths are named after Pacific islands. The drinks come with fruit. It's been there since 1939. What more do you need to know?

Other dives of note include **El Rio** (3158 Mission St., 282-3325), a Bernal Heights haunt with live salsa music, film screenings in summer, and no-budget decor. You have to like a place that advertises itself as "your dive," which El Rio does. Then there's the **Tunnel Top** (601 Bush St., 982-2307), located above the Stockton Street tunnel and the Green Door massage parlor. A tiny place with a Fooseball machine, a squawking TV monitor, and a shattered cocktail sign outside with only the neon olive left intact, the Tunnel Top is a classic city watering hole. At **Spec's** (12 Saroyan Alley, 421-4112), in North Beach, you can eyeball S.F. nostalgia items hung, pinned, and stacked all over the narrow, dark interior, even as the alcohol blurs your vision. **Mr. Bing's Cocktail Lounge** (201 Columbus Ave., 362-1545) is a cramped Chinatown bar with drinks and drinkers who look to have been there since before World War II. Its door is always open, perhaps to lure yuppies from the San Francisco Brewing Company pub across the street, which seems unlikely.

The definitive Chinatown dive is **Li Po** (916 Grant Ave., 982-0072). Amid tourists wandering by in search of "jade" souvenirs and more T-shirts, you enter Li Po through a dank doorway more than one visitor has compared to a cave. Indoors are vinyl booths in the back alcove under multicolored light bulbs, a Buddhist altar with incense and oranges behind the bar, and a big, torn paper lantern overhead, maybe Japanese anime on the TV. Li Po is an old place. *Where to Sin in San Francisco*, an out-of-print book published in 1935, recommends Li Po's reputedly wicked Lychee Blossom cocktail. When I asked a young bartender in a sweat suit if she could make a Lychee Blossom, she looked at me blankly, so I guess the answer was no. Maybe you can get one.

S E C R E T

DOG FRIENDLY

Traveling with your dog? It can be tough to let Fido and Spot run free, given that San Francisco is the second most densely populated American city (after New York), and many San Franciscans understandably frown over the dog litter they encounter around town. All is not lost, however. There are beautiful places to run the dog, places to buy your dog ice cream, even a holistic vet.

The best places for runs — the dog's and yours — are along the waterfront, where there are vast open spaces, soft Mediterranean light, and ocean-fresh air. **Fort Funston** (Skyline, just past John Muir) is the best. It is big, hilly enough for a workout, and dedicated to fun — the city's hang-gliding enthusiasts take off from the bluffs. Another fine place on the water is **Crissy Field**, on the bay just inside the Golden Gate Bridge. The site of San Francisco's first airport back in the days of biplanes, Crissy Field is tabletop flat and pretty, with jogging, bicycling, and walking paths for you and your dog. Just be sure to keep the pooch outside the fenced-in sand dunes, which are being restored with native California flora.

After all that exercise, you and your pet are going to have an appetite. As you relax with a well-earned cone of rocky road or butter brickle, you can get your dog a Pup Cup of vanilla ice cream studded with dog biscuits at **Fountain of Youth** (1484 Church St., 206-9411), an ice cream parlor in Noe Valley. In the Sunset, there's another ice cream opportunity for your dog at **Polly Ann** (3142 Noriega St., 664-2472), which, likewise, is happy to part with a scoop for your pet.

Should all the sweet treats or the stress of travel make your pooch feel poorly, contact **Irving Street Veterinary Hospital** (1434 Irving

St., 664-0191). Homeopathy, chiropractic, acupuncture, and other treatments are available for ailing animals. Northern California is a locus of holistic health care for humans. Why keep it to ourselves?

And let's not forget our feline friends. An all-around interesting pet shop called **George** (2411 California St., 441-0564) sells organic cat-nip for Fluff's recreational pleasure.

Should you want to adopt a pet as a keepsake of your trip to San Francisco, homeless animals are temporarily ensconced at **Maddie's Pet Adoption Center** (250 Florida St., 554-3000) in rooms designed to reflect iconic San Francisco architecture like period Victorian houses. The local SPCA runs this swank facility for dogs, cats, and other critters. But while it looks great, these animals need real homes.

If you want to read all about it, nearby Berkeley is home turf for people who like it ruff. *The Bark* (www.thebark.com or 510-704-0827) is a professionally written and designed national magazine for dog lovers. Nicely balanced between literary musings by the likes of Gertrude Stein and practical information (tips on doggie diets, where to find dog psychologists), the Bark is a bright and frisky quarterly.

SECRET
DOT-COMLAND

In San Francisco, it seems like dot-com Internet culture has conquered the world. It hasn't — yet — but there's no question the Net has combined with the high-tech engines of Silicon Valley to power much of the U.S. economy. Because Internet culture is in essence vir-tual, a good deal of it is online, not on the street. But there are actual, physical gathering places and events for residents of this brave new world, some of which are worth checking out.

The physical epicenter of dot-comland is **South Park** (between Second, Third, Bryant, and Brannan), a small oval greensward laid out in the 1850s and once circled by mansions and the homes of sea captains. The mansions are long gone, replaced by warehouses and workers' apartments built after the originally hilly area was leveled and the looming, roaring Bay Bridge went up in the 1930s. In the 1990s, the area changed again, as light-industrial spaces and warehouses filled up with software companies, e-business ventures, cafes, design studios, and magazine offices. *Wired*, the monthly that celebrates cyberspace and the New Economy, is headquartered at 520 Third Street, though the office can't accommodate visitors. Such is the case in much of the neighborhood, known informally as Multimedia Gulch — a nickname inspired by Silicon Valley, 50 miles south.

It's entirely possible to meet goateed dot-com boys and tattooed and pierced cybergrrrls sitting in South Park on nice days with their laptops, Palm Pilots, coffee, and fresh-cut sandwiches from **Caffe Centro** (102 South Park, 882-1500). If you want to eat inside, go to **Ristorante Ecco** (101 South Park, 495-3291) for Italian cuisine and next-table-over deal-making talk, or **South Park Cafe** (108 South Park, 495-7275), a charming, small, French-style cafe with unpretentious fresh food and good coffee.

Bars are as uncommon in South Park as rotary telephones. **Infusion** (555 Second St., 543-2282) serves food but is most admired for its namesake vodka infusions made with fruit. Multimedia Gulch — don't look for a real gulch, there isn't one — sprawls as far as a mile westward, to Ninth Street or so. Another hip bar, closer to the western border, is **330 Ritch** (330 Ritch St., 541-9574), a hideaway on a nondescript alley.

With all the venture capital money flying around, dot-commers have the budgets and the hubris to party a lot, which they do — starting Wednesday and Thursday nights. Indeed, the best way to jack into this work-hard, play-hard crowd is to party with them. If you can't get in on their stock options, you can at least get a drink from the fully hosted bar. Dot-com party info is posted online or sent out via e-mail. Check www.sfgirl.com, a Web site run by entrepreneur Patty Beron, a.k.a. SFGirl, for launch party postings and dot-com gossip. The **Industry Standard** (315 Pacific Ave.), a bright, successful weekly magazine that tracks the Internet economy, hosts rooftop cocktail parties at its office every Friday after work at 5 p.m. You need an invitation to get in. If you get in, tell *Industry Standard* publisher John Battelle I said hi. He's a smart, sociable, thirtysomething guy with tiny eyeglasses. Battelle was my main editor when I freelanced for *Wired*.

You have a better chance of crashing a dot-com party if you're female and have a business card to give out when you get there than you'll have otherwise.

SECRET
EARTHQUAKES

Earthquakes happen. There's nothing secret about the 'quakes themselves, of course. The '06 Big One registered a monstrous 8.3 on the Richter scale and devastated the city, making worldwide headlines. The '89 Pretty Big One was a 7.1 Richter bounce that shook things up plenty while television crews were in town for the World Series. You're almost certainly not going to be in a major earthquake while

you're visiting, but it's easy to get rattled and not know what to do should the ground start to move and assert itself. If you're indoors, duck under something heavy, like a desk, or stand in a doorframe. Don't flip any switches right away, and don't light candles or cigarettes. Outdoors, get away from power lines and windows. If you're driving, pull over and stop.

There's almost too much information at this Web site, but if you feel you're not quake wise, check out the **U.S. Geological Survey's** site at quake.wr.usgs.gov.

SECRET
FIERY FOODS

Some like it hot, and those people are in luck in this town, where Asian and Latin American markets abound in red-hot chili peppers and spicy curries, and restaurant cooks can push the boundaries of your tolerance for heat. When I was a kid growing up far from multicultural San Francisco, bland was in. We avoided spices, using nothing more adventurous than black pepper and salt. As a wannabe sophisticate during my university years, my philosophy was "the hotter the better." My friends and I competed to show how far we had come from our conservative backgrounds by eating the most scalding food possible and pretending we liked it. It was a new form of macho. Later, I concluded that heat should enhance the flavor of food, not overpower it. You can find fiery foods done right in many places around town, none better than these.

New Golden Turtle (308 Fifth Ave., 221-5285) is a budget-saving, palate-pleasing Vietnamese neighborhood restaurant in the inner Richmond that makes superior coconut chicken soup with just the right amount of heat and lemongrass chicken with plenty of red chilis, chicken, sesame seeds, and a dash of soy sauce. No atmosphere whatsoever, but very good food.

Khan Toke Thai House (5937 Geary Blvd., 668-6654), in the outer Richmond, is a tradition-minded place where fluffy steamed rice is served in silver bowls. You remove your shoes before entering and sit at low tables. Tell them how hot you want it. There's always a bit of sweet heat to wake up the taste buds.

San Francisco Bar-B-Q (1328 18th St., 431-8956) serves forth spicy-hot Thai barbeque and other savory items without any formal trappings. You can eat like a king for $10, or start your own dynasty for $15, at this modest Potrero Hill neighborhood favorite.

At **La Cumbre** (515 Valencia St., 863-8205), a primo Mexican taqueria in the Mission district, the prices are low enough to bring a tear to your eye. The food may do the same. Again, tell them how hot you want it when you reach the front of the line — there's no table service — and they say "hot sauce?"

The seventh heaven of hot is the **Hunan Restaurant** (924 Sansome St., 956-7727), once a cramped lunch counter that *The New Yorker* magazine called "the best Chinese restaurant in the world." That's a mouthful, of course, but the Hunan is very good. It was hot commercially for a while, too. The foodies moved on in search of the next trend, as they are wont to do, after the Hunan moved into a warehouse-sized space. It's still incredibly good. I favor the Henry's Special: sautéed scallops, chicken, carrots, chilis, green beans, and bamboo shoots, washed down with a bottle of Pilsner Urquell. The Hunan will hold the salt and MSG if you ask, but the traces of fire in the food ensure that it's tingly and flavorful, and never, ever bland.

S E C R E T
FITNESS

As the local joke has it, San Franciscans keep biking, jogging, power walking, power lifting, and whatever else they can think of to take off the weight they put on at power lunches. It's no joke. You see people putting on and taking off the same 15 pounds. Fitness centers compete fiercely for the taking-off part, offering gleaming gyms with water views and the latest high-tech gimmicks, up to and including stationary bicycles with e-mail.

Working out, like working itself, takes place round the clock in the information age. Witness the blossoming of — at last count — nine San Francisco locations for **24 Hour Fitness**. Like San Francisco's ubiquitous street people, fitness centers are becoming so thick on the ground that you don't have to find them. They'll find you.

Big names like **Gold's Gym** and **Crunch** are muscling into the market, but San Franciscans are often partial to non-profit enterprises and their neighborhood gyms. **The Embarcadero YMCA** (169 Steuart St., 957-9622) has a state-of-the-art facility with lovely bay views that opened up after the neighboring freeway was demolished in 1991. Weights, aerobics — whatever you want, the Y has it. It also has a dedicated racquetball phone line (957-1770), if you want to check the availability of a court. **Valencia Street Muscle & Fitness** (333 Valencia St., 626-8360) is a popular, well-equipped gym in the Mission district that advertises itself thusly: "Face it, your gym sucks."

But suppose you can't kick the e-mail drug, can't bear to be disconnected at any time, even while working out. No sweat. Many of the fitness centers around town feature Netpulse Exercise Bikes. These stationary bicycles have screens that allow you to surf the Net, get your e-mail, watch cable TV, and whatever the manufacturer thinks of next, so long as you keep pedaling, keep pedaling, keep pedaling.

That sounds far too connected, to me. I prefer old-fashioned, low-tech jogging out of doors in the mild weather and fresh air. **Crissy Field**, the **Embarcadero**, and other waterfront locales are fine places to run. Another place, usually not crowded and always beautiful, is the oval track at the **Polo Field** in **Golden Gate Park**. Graceful, pleasant-smelling eucalyptus trees ring the track, and there's often a game going on in the infield below: usually soccer, sometimes rugby or lacrosse. The track is packed clay, which can get muddy after winter rains but is otherwise a good surface. Keep an eye out for the occasional cantering horse and rider; the park stables are just north of the track.

SECRET
FOG
⚜

I was going to tell you everything about the fog, about how it forms when hot summer air in California's Central Valley pulls cool marine air inland, and how that makes the city 30 degrees cooler in July than inland places 30 miles away, and how a San Franciscan can't get to sleep without hearing the mournful baritone of the foghorn on Alcatraz Island, and how the fog looks like dry ice as it pours over the Marin headlands and grabs the Golden Gate Bridge in its chilly embrace, and how it really looks incredibly like snow as it blows

through the trees in Buena Vista Park but more like rain lashed by wind through the trees of Lincoln Park, and how the fogbank always seems to break right at Masonic Avenue in late morning leaving the west side of the city cool and gray and the east side warm and sunny, and that there must be 40 businesses with the word "fog" or "fog city" in them, and that the town's leading rock radio station uses KFOG as its call letters, and why you feel you're in a Dashiell Hammett mystery when you watch the fog swirl around the neon marquee of the Vogue Theater, and why the fog is precisely why most people in San Francisco don't have or need air conditioning, and how the temperature dropped from 98 degrees to 65 in an hour one afternoon when the fog came in and broke the back of an October heat wave and I felt the fog before I saw it as the cool breeze blew through the open door and down the hall in a friend's Mission district shotgun flat. But then I thought, "What the heck is really secret about the summer fog? Maybe they're not interested in this anyway, and I should write about something else." So, I'll get back to you about the fog.

S E C R E T
FOOTWEAR

Let's say you are a drag queen or a prostitute. Okay. Let's say you know someone who is a drag queen or perhaps a prostitute — not that they're the same thing, or bad things. Right. Let's say you're going to a costume party, and you're dressing up, and you'd like something, uh, a little different, and footwear is very important to you. What to do? Where to go?

Two words: **Foot Worship** (1214 Sutter St., 921-FOOT). This shop in the racy, seedy Tenderloin is frequented, in part, by actual drag queens and — it is reported — actual prostitutes, who want something a little different, too. Like stiletto heels five inches high, even eight inches high. Or thigh-high boots. Stuff like that — stuff that cross-dressers, dancers, and other folks like, too. Remember the name: Foot Worship. Remember the number: 921-FOOT. That's 921-FOOT. Operators — or at least voicemail — are standing by.

On the other hand, suppose you want footwear that has nothing — that's nothing — to do with fetishes or bad, possibly illegal, behavior. And you want it custom made for your feet because shoes and boots never really fit you, and you're *you*, an individual with specific needs. What to do? Where to go?

One word: **Mapuche** (500 Laguna St., 551-0725). Mapuche, in the increasingly hip Hayes Valley neighborhood, custom-makes shoes as you like 'em. No, they're not cheap. Yes, they are unique. They're you.

SECRET
FRANCOPHILIA

It's no exaggeration to say that San Francisco has a crush on France and, especially, its romantic capital city. Indeed, planeloads of socialites and civic leaders are forever jetting off to Paris on junkets to do some very important work on one project or another. Beyond that, many San Franciscans — and not just rich and semi-famous ones — have done their best to re-create a bit of the City of Light in the city by the bay. They've done it pretty well.

The centers of Francophilia are the alleyways and cafes downtown near Bush Street and Grant Avenue. **Cafe de la Presse** (352 Grant Ave., 398-2680) serves freshly baked croissants, heady coffee, and freshly squeezed orange juice in the morning, along with a good selection of international magazines, and has a dining room with a fine wine list. Within a few blocks is **Cafe Claude** (7 Claude Lane, 392-3505), which sets out tables on fine days and serves straight-ahead, hearty French fare. **Cafe Bastille** (22 Belden Place, 986-5673) is an informal eatery on two levels on another alleyway. It likewise sets out tables for open-air dining, as does its near neighbor **Plouf** (40 Belden Place, 986-6491). Plouf sparkles with white linen and gleaming wine glasses, and serves scrumptious seafood entrees, the specialty of the house; try the mussels. On Bastille Day, tiny Belden Place and Claude Lane are cordoned off. DJs set up turntables for heavily amplified disco beats, and far too many people squeeze into these small places and drink far too much. Pinned in by the tide of humanity, I feel like an aristocrat of the *ancien régime* being hauled before the guillotine. The rest of the year, these are civilized little lanes with civilized, palatable restaurants.

Some of the city's most accomplished and elegant restaurants have French accents: Fleur de Lys, Masa's, Charles of Nob Hill, Le Central, the Fifth Floor, and Berkeley's citadel of nouvelle cuisine, Chez Panisse. These places are famous and prosperous, and rightly so.

Off the well-trod path, you can find good French food at lower prices and, sometimes, with far shorter waiting times for reservations. Booking at the big-name places, by contrast, can feel like a food fight.

Curbside Too (2769 Lombard St., 921-4442) is an intimate branch of the popular **Curbside Cafe** (2417 California St., 929-9030) and is even more enjoyable. Situated at the eastern gate of the Presidio, Curbside Too serves succulent French food at moderate prices, and who could argue with that? If it's too busy, go around the corner and try the robust pub fare at **Liverpool Lil's** (2942 Lyon St., 921-6664), a rollicking bar and restaurant. **Jeanne d'Arc** (715 Bush St., 421-3154) has low-key charm and a country French menu. Located downstairs in the Hotel Cornell, it's not well known beyond hotel guests and nearby office workers, but it should be.

Near downtown on an unappetizing block of Fifth Street is **Le Charm** (315 Fifth St., 546-6128), a bustling bistro that makes you forget anything unappetizing as soon as you step in the door. The pommes frites are great, as are the poultry and meat dishes, and there's a comfortable courtyard out back for sunny-day dining. In Hayes Valley, near City Hall, **Absinthe Restaurant & Bar** (398 Hayes St., 551-1590) is another charmer. Lined with vintage French posters and photos, and fronted by big windows, it serves hearty portions (though not the lethal drink it's named for). **Clementine** (126 Clement St., 387-0408) brings unforced grace to a workaday block in the inner Richmond. The city's best Breton-style crepes can be found at **Ti Couz** (3108 16th St., 252-7373), a very cool and very good place that serves both sweet dessert crepes and lovely savory crepes big enough and good enough to be the centerpiece of a full meal. And the city's best soufflés are at **Cafe Jacqueline** (1454 Grant Ave., 981-5565), a small, very French, dinner-only spot in the heart of Italian North Beach.

If you hunger for more than French food, visit the center of French language and culture, the **Alliance Française** (1345 Bush St., 775-7755), in its elegant gated complex on a hardscrabble stretch of Bush Street, or buy a French book or periodical at the **French Bookstore of San Francisco** (925 Larkin St., 474-0626). The newspaper of the local francophone community is *Journal Français* (1051 Divisadero St., 921-5100).

SECRET

FREE DRINKS

Look, there are two ways to get drinks. One is by paying for them. Another is by getting them free. Which do you prefer? Thought so. So…

Head toward the ocean, give your name at the door at the **Pacific Cafe** (7000 Geary Blvd., 387-7091), and join the queue. While you're waiting — anywhere from 20 minutes to more than an hour on weekends and holidays — a waiter will come round and fill your glass with white jug wine. If it's crowded, you may wait outside on the sidewalk. No matter. It's a very convivial scene. People sip, chat, and make new friends. By the time you squeeze into the small, cheery, woody dining room for the decent but not great seafood, you're hungry and feeling cheery yourself. There's no extra charge for the wine and you can have as much as you want until you're seated. This is a warm, neighborhood restaurant with a citywide draw. Many of the employees have been there for years, and many patrons are long-standing regulars. The Pacific Cafe doesn't take reservations, which helps account for the line.

Another fun thing to do is to make the downtown art gallery scene for **First Thursday** (the first Thursday night of every month), when many galleries near Union Square pour free wine at opening receptions and San Franciscans walk from gallery to gallery. You might start out at **49 Geary Street**, a downtown building honeycombed with galleries. Things start at 5 p.m. and go for two or three hours. Go early. It is crowded but sociable and it's a great way to see art.

Or, you could check out the art of brewing by doing the free tour and tasting at **Anchor Brewing Company** (1705 Mariposa St., 863-

8350). The dean of American microbrewers, washing machine heir Fritz Maytag, has been making his world-class Anchor Steam Beer, Liberty Ale, Old Foghorn barley wine ale, and other hoppy, slightly bubbly brews since the late 1960s, when he saved Anchor, in business since 1896, from sinking into oblivion by buying it. The tour is informative and fun, and the brewery — with Art Deco touches on the outside and a showcase tap room festooned with brewing memorabilia inside — looks immaculate and smells incredibly good. Open, 250-pound bags of hops account for the great smells, along with malt. At the end of the 30-minute tour, the payoff arrives. You get to quaff half-sized glasses of six Anchor products. Call for reservations. Tours are held weekdays at 2 p.m.

SECRET
FREE MUSIC

In gray, rainy winter, when you really need it, you can find music for free, if you know where to look. Usually, that means going to church — not during services, but for the free concerts several churches bestow on the city. There are fine classical concerts at **Old St. Mary's Cathedral** (660 California St., 288-3800), built in 1854; **Old First Presbyterian Church** (1751 Sacramento St., 474-1608); **First Unitarian Universalist Church** (1187 Franklin St., 776-4580); and **St. Patrick's Church** (756 Mission St., 777-3211). **St. Mary's Cathedral**, a huge, towering structure opened in 1970 (1111 Gough St., 567-3775) specializes in organ concerts. The music is usually classical, and usually good, and the price is certainly right. You can make a

donation if you wish, of course. Specifics are in the local papers, notably the *Chronicle*'s Datebook section and the weeklies.

If you're in town during the summer months, you'll have many more opportunities to hear free sounds and the variety of music will be correspondingly greater. The Embarcadero Center, that cluster of wafer-thin high-rises downtown between Clay, Sacramento, Battery, and Drumm streets, hosts a **Summer Jazz Series** (772-0734 or www.sfjazz.org). Performances are usually held outdoors on the promenade level of Embarcadero Two at midday. The biggest and most ambitious musical lineup is presented by the Market Street Association's **People in Plazas** program (362-2500 or www.marketstreet. citysearch.com). Jazz, swing, Afro-Cuban, country, blues, Latin sounds, Celtic airs, hot Dixieland — all can be heard free at nine downtown outdoor venues. The program runs from early June through the end of September. Bring a lunch or lay back with a latte. This series has been going on annually since 1976.

For long-lived tradition, check out the free concerts at the **Golden Gate Park band shell** in the park's main concourse, also held in summer at 1 p.m. on Sundays. San Francisco's municipal band has been playing there since 1882. These free al fresco concerts are charmingly retro, resolutely mainstream, and family-friendly.

SECRET
GARDENS

To find San Francisco's secret gardens, go in and up. Some of the loveliest gardens are hidden on the roofs of downtown office towers.

One of the best is on the seventh floor of One Market Plaza's **Spear Tower** (One Market Plaza), near the Ferry Building and not far from the Bay Bridge. Tables and chairs ring a central green and, of course, there are flowers. It's a restful spot in a very businesslike part of the city. Another fine roof garden blossoms on the fifteenth floor of **343 Sansome Street**, in an office tower built in 1908. There are blooms aplenty, as well as potted olive trees and a view of the once-despised but now iconic Transamerica Pyramid. You'll find office workers brown-bagging it, reading, or chatting up the colleague from the next cubicle. Not many people aside from the denizens of the buildings know about these two gardens, both of which are open to the public.

If you prefer to keep your feet on the ground but don't object to having an urban alpine experience, walk up two steep blocks to the **Vallejo Street Garden**. You start at the bottom of Vallejo and Montgomery streets and climb the outdoor steps. Many people don't care to go vertical if it means exerting themselves. More's the pity for them and the better for you, as this flowery spot with inspiring views of San Francisco Bay will probably be somewhat empty.

Golden Gate Park is big enough to have many special spots, including lovely gardens. At the western end of the park by the ocean is the colorful **Queen Wilhelmina Tulip Garden**, located next to the Dutch Windmill. The tulip garden was dedicated by the Queen of the Netherlands, and then more or less fell off the map after all the initial fuss. People who find their way there always appear mellow, and no one seems to mind if you discreetly use the soft grass near the flower beds as a make-out spot.

Near the east end of Golden Gate Park is the **Shakespeare Garden**, planted with flowers, trees, and herbs named in Shakespeare's poetry and plays. People use this small, bucolic place to sit quietly on the benches and catch up on their reading. Benches are dedicated to people who loved this spot, often people in the arts. One bench bears the following dedication to Bill Ball, founder of the American Conservatory Theater, from Steve Silver, impresario of S.F.'s long-running musical farce *Beach Blanket Babylon*: "Bill Ball — for his encouragement, artistry, and genius." A wall at the southern end of the garden carries quotations from the Bard. "I know a bank whereon the wild thyme blooms, where oxlips and the nodding violet grows, quite over-canopied with luscious woodbine, with sweet musk-roses, and with eglantine . . ." This is a garden for dreaming with eyes open.

SECRET
GAY
✂

San Francisco was a gay mecca a long time before businesses began displaying the rainbow flag. Subterranean scenes for gay men and lesbians existed back in the 19th century, when the city was being born in the fever of the Gold Rush, and were well established by the 1950s. In the 1970s, the "subterranean" part was discarded as repressive and old-fashioned, and the scene developed in an incredible variety of ways and in impressively short order. Nowadays, in addition to the events and institutions that engage nearly all gay men and lesbians, such as the Names Project's AIDS Memorial Quilt, the beautiful James C. Hormel Gay and Lesbian Center in the Main Library, and the — deep breath — San Francisco Lesbian, Gay, Bisexual, Transgender Pride Celebration Parade held every June, highly specific niches have been carved out. (Also see Secret Lesbian.)

Take, for example, the **Bear Store** (367 Ninth St., 552-1506). The Bear Store is not a bargain outlet for actual, ursine-type bears, but for bear-like gay men. Big guys. Round guys. Hairy guys. Husky guys. Big, round, hairy, husky guys who want to buy, say, leather chaps, a vest, or some other bear-friendly attire, and want to do it at a place that knows what they're interested in, what they'll look good in, and what they'll feel good in. Thus, the Bear Store.

Or, let's say a bear wants some rough and tumble action. Possibly, a bear on the prowl could be readily accommodated at **Martuni's** (4 Valencia St., 241-0205), but Martuni's — a bar known for its elegant, icy martinis — is a refined, Noel Coward kind of place. Perhaps a more likely venue for bear fun would be the rough and ready **Hole in the Wall** (289 Eighth St., 431-4695), where no pretense of refinement is made, or **The Stud** (399 Ninth St., 252-7883), a long-time gay favorite whose name says it all. Even The Stud offers variety, though. On Tuesdays, the club hosts a special showcase for flamboyant drag queens — if "flamboyant drag queens" isn't redundant — called Trannyshack.

Indeed, specificity abounds. **Este Noche** (3079 16th St., 861-5757) is a cabaret for Latino transsexuals who do both lip-synched and live shows. Even non-trannies have to like Este Noche's happy hour, which is five hours long, going from 4 p.m. to 9 p.m. **The Endup** (401 Sixth St., 357-0827) has been a mostly gay dance club for some time; on Fridays it goes way gay with "Fag Fridays," which actually last until 6 a.m. Saturdays. On Saturday nights, the gay gym all-stars take over for a themed night of shirtless dancing called Club Universe at **Club Townsend** (177 Townsend St., 974-1156), when cartoonishly buff men flex and strut. It's gay with a twang at **Rawhide** (280 Seventh St., 621-1197), another dance club, this one a country & western thing. Asian drag queens — oops, "gender illusionists" —

serve food and drinks and lip-synch pop hits at **AsiaSF** (201 Ninth St., 255-2742).

After all that, a hungry bear or non-bear can chow down at **Hamburger Mary's** (1582 Folsom St., 626-1985), a gay institution since the 1970s. Hamburger Mary's serves breakfast all day, has a well-used poolroom, and puts milk on the table in bottles with rubber nipples. Not an inch of the place goes undecorated. I did a dinner interview for the *Examiner* with gay activist Tom Ammiano there when he was ramping up his political career. As we settled in to do the interview, he ordered a Blue Hawaii, a cocktail that is, of course, blue. I asked Ammiano what was in it, and what made it blue. "I don't know," he said with mock perplexity. "Windex?" A few years later, Ammiano ran for mayor, forced a run-off, and got 40 percent of the vote, so there may be some secret ingredient in Hamburger Mary's cocktails after all.

S E C R E T
GOLF

Not to be too terribly contentious, but I've always been fond of the old description of golf as "a good walk spoiled." Except that now, with the advent of hurry-up motorized golf carts, golfers with cell phones traipsing the fairways, and who knows what next, you'd have to call it a good ride spoiled. The appeal of golf remains unfathomable to me, but I have trusted friends and dearly beloved relatives who are in thrall to the Scottish game, so go figure. Golf is, of course, played in San Francisco. The city has four public courses, one of which is worth walking or riding around for the views alone. You can rent stuff at all of them.

Golden Gate Park (Fulton St. and 47th Ave., 751-8987) has a tidy, nine-hole course at par 27. **Harding Park** (Skyline Blvd. and Harding Rd. at Lake Merced, 664-4690) has two courses: a nine-hole course that is a par 32, and an 18-hole, par 72 course. The **Presidio golf course** (Arguello at Findley, 561-4664) was built back in 1896 for duffers in the officer corps of the U.S. Army, and then opened to the public in the 1990s. It's the only public golf course in a national park. Renovated in 2000, it is a 6,589-yard, par 72 course with Bentgrass greens, which I am given to understand are snazzy, indeed.

However, the crown jewel of the city's public courses is the non-trendy, gorgeous **Lincoln Park course** (34th Ave. at Clement St., 221-9911). Lincoln Park covers 5,081 yards and is a par 72. It has a decidedly modest clubhouse, a fairly cheesy restaurant, and no pretensions at all. It's a place for the hoi polloi to make like Tiger Woods, and that's endearing. But beyond that, Lincoln Park undulates over acres of grassy bluffs with smashing views of the Pacific and San Francisco Bay, and, gleaming between them, the Golden Gate Bridge. The panorama from the 17th hole is simply awe inspiring. Even if you don't play, it may be worth risking the occasional airborne ball to catch that view. Afterwards, you can do something worthwhile, like head up the hill to the Palace of the Legion of Honor to visit the museum's Rodin collection. Hey, nothing against golf.

SECRET
GREASY SPOONS

Greasy spoon eateries perform several worthy functions. They give you the occasional case of food poisoning, thus honing your survival skills. They're often open at odd hours — very early, say, or very late, or all the time — which comes in handy when the munchies won't be denied. They serve the comfort food everyone knows and almost everyone wants from time to time. And they're cheap, a virtue not to be underestimated in a city as expensive as San Francisco.

Art's Cafe (747 Irving St., 665-7440) is a contender for cheapest restaurant in San Francisco. A hole in the wall lunch counter that serves lunch and breakfast, Art's has a breakfast special — two eggs, two pieces of sausage or bacon, and two pancakes — for $2.65. You can get breakfast until 2:30 p.m. There are no tables or chairs; you sit on stools at a counter inlaid with postcards from all over the world. Art's serves mostly basic American fare, with hash brown potatoes woven into a mass as firm as a rubber welcome mat and industrial-strength coffee. But several Asian dishes, including chicken teriyaki and eggs served over rice in a huge bowl, are good, and service in this family-run place is friendly.

Bill's Place (2315 Clement St., 221-5262) has lost a little of its designer cachet since the American flag that used to hang on the wall behind the register has come down, but the burgers, fries, pies, and ice cream are still there, still intensely caloric, and still cheap. The thick chocolate shakes are great, and must be spooned down. **Joe's Coffee Shop** (6134 Geary Blvd., 668-9382) is your basic one-stop for pancakes, hash browns, eggs as you like 'em, and strong coffee. Run by an Asian family, it's a tiny place with a TV monitor on top of the listing fridge and a sunny front window usually occupied by couples, while singles and folks who want to chat up the owners sit at the counter. **Harvey's Place** (330 Fifth St., 495-0448), a combination lunch counter, five-and-dime, grocery, and liquor store, is a bike messenger hangout where the burgers and packaged junk food are cheap, and the ambience is funky. The **Pork Store Cafe** (1451 Haight St.,

864-6981) attracts a rough-hewn Haight-Ashbury crowd for basic vittles. At **Louis'** (902 Point Lobos Ave., 387-6330), S.F. cops, gaggles of out-of-towners who wander up the hill from the Cliff House, and locals who want a filling breakfast cram into a small space with big windows and dramatic views of the ocean. The omelets are leaden and the service inattentive, but the views and eclectic mix of customers are interesting.

In the très trendy SOMA (South of Market) district, **Butter** (354 11th St., 863-5964) bills itself as a "white-trash bistro" and serves only food that can be heated in a microwave. Butter is mostly a bar, with DJs at night. But it serves starchy, sugary foodstuffs from a kitchen installed in a 1950s trailer that is, in turn, parked inside Butter's bright-yellow building. Of course, Butter is winking at you. Figures that a society that favors faux marble, facsimile documents, and virtual relationships would like mock greasy spoons, too. But the macaroni and cheese, Swanson TV Dinners, and Tater Tots are real, and you can wash them down with the house special: vodka and Red Bull energy drink.

In what may be America's most Asian-influenced city, one of the city's prime greasy spoons is the Vietnamese restaurant **Tu Lan** (8 Sixth St., 626-0927). Located on a scummy block of Skid Row with drunken crazies outside and less than sparkling sanitation inside, Tu Lan can be challenging. But its deep-fried imperial rolls are crunchy and flavorful, the Vietnamese coffee is a perfect blend of roasted beans and sweet condensed milk, and the stir-fried vegetables are terrific. In the late 1980s, the *Examiner*'s food and wine writer, Jim Wood, took famous foodie Julia Child to this intensely downmarket spot for lunch. As Child literally stepped over a drunk on the sidewalk, Wood's story goes, the fellow woke up, looked up, and recognized her. "Bon appetit," he croaked.

S E C R E T

HATS

Sometimes there's a need to keep the sun out of your eyes or the rain out of your hair. Sometimes you just want to look good. Maybe you need a hat. If so, and if you're also looking for good value, head to **Kaplan's Surplus & Sporting Goods** (1055 Market St., 863-3486). Located near downtown on an unappetizing stretch of Market, Kaplan's is fine on the inside, especially if you have an appetite for military surplus headgear and want to save a few bucks. More discounted hats are on offer at **California Surplus** (1541 Haight St., 861-0404), which stocks military surplus and the ever-popular Kangol line.

San Francisco is misty and chilly in winter, a season when wool hats and caps can come in handy, indeed. **Irish Castle Gift Shop** (537 Geary St., 474-7432) has caps suitable for the weather; they know misty and chilly in Ireland. There's also a small but good selection of wool caps at **Irish Imports** (3244 Geary Blvd., 752-0961).

Brides looking for wedding hats have a fine chance of finding something distinctive to wear when bells are ringing at **Coup de Chapeau** (1821 Steiner St., 931-7793). The mayor of San Francisco, Willie Brown, complements his Brioni suits with sharp Borsalinos and other hats from **Mrs. Dewson's Hats** (2050 Fillmore St., 346-1600). Should you want a great new Stetson to go with those numerous head of cattle you just acquired in Abilene, the place to go is **Stetson Western Hats** (2629 Taylor St., 441-1187), which also sells a wide range of Western gear for cowboys and cowgirls. And cats and kitties in search of vintage headgear that will look good in the cocktail lounge and on the swing-dancing floor should check out **Martini**

Mercantile (1773 Haight St., 668-3746), which offers gear for all your retro needs.

Several places in town offer custom-made hats. You'll pay more for them, of course, but you'll also get a hat that fits perfectly and flatters your sense of style. **Kingsley Hat Studio** (3404 Balboa Ave., 387-8838) rolls their own — er, makes fine, custom-designed hats for men and women. **Paul's Hat Works** (6128 Geary Blvd., 221-5332) is an elegant little shop in the outer Richmond that specializes in stylish white Panama hats, sold in a small space festooned with Tiffany lamps and copies of *Cigar Aficionado* magazine. The material is hand-woven in Ecuador, then hand blocked, stitched, and crafted by S.F. custom hatter Michael Harris. Paul's is a masculine place in an old-time way that recalls dark-wood private libraries with deep carpets and arm-chairs where you can sit for hours reading Gibbon.

The most outrageous hats in sight are on the heads of the performers in *Beach Blanket Babylon*, a raunchy musical farce (Club Fugazi, 678 Green St., 421-4222) that has been running forever. You can see the Golden Gate Bridge, Coit Tower, the Transamerica Pyramid, and other local landmarks reproduced in three dimensions atop one very tall, very broad hat. Of course, these hats aren't for sale.

SECRET

HAWAIIAN

Hawaii is tropical, rainy, hot, lightly populated, and laid back. San Francisco is temperate, dry save for mid-winter, cool, densely popu-lated, and theoretically laid back but not really. So, naturally, these two places are linked.

Some of the linkage is geographical. San Francisco is a prime transfer point for mainlanders and international travelers going to and from Hawaii. But several tens of thousands of islanders have also moved to the Bay Area in search of jobs and new lives, bringing their food, slack-key guitar music, and hospitable aloha spirit. Much of the local scene is private, but some former islanders operate businesses and an annual Aloha Festival takes place each summer.

You can find a savory, upscale version of Hawaiian food at **Tita's Hale' Aina** (3870 17th St., 626-2477). Tita's is spic and span, fragrant with aromas from the kitchen, and cheery; indeed, the menu advises patrons, "If you are in a rush, we strongly recommend you hang loose." Tita's Kalua pig and cabbage cooked in ti leaves is intensely flavorful, and its coco mac prawns — prawns dipped in coconut, served with macadamia nuts and mango chutney — are delicious. The corned beef hash is made with taro root. Tita's doesn't serve alcohol, but it does have lau lau the last Friday of every month: pork, chicken, and salmon in taro leaves wrapped in ti leaves and steamed for seven hours.

Most S.F. Hawaiian places are very down home. **Punahele Island Grill** (2650 Judah Ave., 759-8276) has long, family-style tables, an altar piled with gourds under a skylight, and warm service. It figures: a help-wanted sign when I was last there specified that applicants "must have aloha spirit." Christmas lights wink overhead, and there is a small stage for nighttime karaoke. I like the Punahele for breakfast. Good omelets with Portuguese sausage come island-style with steamed rice. At **Hawaiian Drive-In No. 28** (4827 Mission St., 586-9382), you can find an even humbler version of Hawaiian "local food" — plate lunches with macaroni salad, steamed rice, and meat, possibly Spam. Hawaiian Drive-In No. 28 is actually a tiny restaurant, not a drive-in. It has three tables, large portions, and low prices.

To feed the soul — and to read the posters and leaflets to find out what is going on — local Hawaiians check out the **Hawaii Store** (2655 Judah Ave., 566-0111). The small shop functions as a de facto social and cultural center, selling CDs and tapes of Hawaiian music, aloha shirts, soft drinks like Hawaii Gold strawberry and guava, and taro chips. I think it's no coincidence that the Hawaii Store is in the outer Sunset district. It allows islanders to see the ocean and let their thoughts sail west.

If your thoughts of the island take flight on drink and grub, stop in at the geographically challenged **Hawaii West** cocktail lounge (729 Vallejo St., 362-3220), knock one back at the tiki bar under the Waikiki Beach sign, and, if you dare, gently let slip that S.F. is actually east of Hawaii.

Another source of information on all things Hawaiian for locals and visitors is the ***Kapalakiko Productions Newsletter*** (800 Meade Ave., 468-7125), which ballyhoos the Aloha Festival and helps islanders and their friends network year round.

SECRET
HERB CAEN

Once upon a time, there was a city of romance and style, where handsome men wore sharply creased suits and fedoras, beautiful women were beautifully coiffed and wore white gloves, the wine was newly opened, and the crabs were newly pulled from the bay. This was a city that existed in reality to a certain degree, and endured for years in idealized form in the newspaper columns of Herb Caen, San Francisco's greatest journalist.

Caen, who wrote a daily column in the *Chronicle* for most of the 59 years from 1938 until his death in 1997, told San Franciscans a story about themselves that he embroidered over and over. Thousands of people learned how to become San Franciscans in no small part by reading his tales of the city. For this, he was loved. When Caen celebrated his 80th birthday in 1996, 75,000 people partied with him outside on the Embarcadero, and bars all over town sold vodka martinis for 75 cents, the 1938 price. It was Caen's favorite drink. Nowadays, a promenade on the Embarcadero is known as **Herb Caen Way...** in his honor. The ellipses in the street signs were inspired by the three dots that separated items in Caen's column.

A few other physical items remain. The *Chronicle* displays Caen's typewriter, a Royal manual — he refused to give it up for a computer — in its ornate lobby with its vaulted ceilings (901 Mission St.). A goodly number of local journalists also cherish the letters he sent them when they wrote something he liked. I still have mine, dated 1989.

But the lamentable truth is, tangible mementos of Caen are few in number. Herb would understand.

In 1988, he wrote that San Francisco is "a marvelous city to write about. Like a snake, it sheds its skin, changes its shape, wanders off in unexpected directions. A hard city for sentimentalists, which most writers are. Beloved landmarks disappear, manners and mores change, 'unforgettable' characters die and are forgotten."

As if to prove the point, a mural on Mission Street showing a beatific Caen presiding over San Francisco from heaven was obliterated by gentrification when a new building went up next to it maybe a year after it was painted. Too bad. But Caen was a writer. He's best remembered, or first encountered, by reading him. Used bookstores sometimes cough up books of his collected columns. Among them are *Baghdad-by-the-Bay* and *One Man's San Francisco*. If you see them, buy them. You won't get the faded topical references, but that won't matter. Their value is in the timeless writing, the soul.

SECRET
HERBS

Back when San Francisco was a village in the remote Mexican province of Alta California, it was called Yerba Buena: "good herb." Subsequently, the little village grew up and changed its name, but it has always retained its link with herbs — the kind you drink in tea, take in capsules or tablets, and smoke in pipes and funny cigarettes. Today, it is a dynamic center for the medicinal and culinary use of herbs. Its multicultural population ensures that Asian, Native American, African-Caribbean, and European herbal traditions contribute to a rich mix, along with more recent arrivals from the New Age counterculture.

In 2000, there were no fewer than 103 entries under Herbs in the San Francisco Yellow Pages, encompassing herb shops, importers, health food stores, doctors, and other health care providers. Most are Chinese herb shop-cum-groceries and medical offices that mix herbal medicine with other disciplines, such as acupuncture. If you speak Chinese or know someone who does, you will make out better.

My favorite place to browse is the **World Ginseng Center** (801 Kearny St., 362-0928). It seems rather grandly named to me, after having seen an entire department store devoted to traditional Chinese medicine in downtown Shanghai, but I still like this bright, clean, well-lit shop that throws open its doors to passersby. Just walking by, you can catch the earthy, slightly musty smell from thousands of ginseng roots that are boxed, stacked, and otherwise displayed. Price tags can top $100 for rare Korean roots with their man-like shape.

Dozens of Asian medical offices practice herbal medicine. They tend to be concentrated in old Chinatown and the newer Chinatown along Clement Street. Again, it helps if you or someone you know speaks Chinese, and it might pay to look for a shop with licensed medical doctors on staff. The **American College of Traditional Chinese Medicine** (450 Connecticut St., 282-9603) offers a free clinic where senior instructors supervise students who check out walk-ins. **Quan Yin Healing Arts Center** (455 Valencia St., 861-4964) taps traditional Chinese medicine, including herbs, to treat serious conditions, including HIV. The **Acupuncture Immune Enhancement Project** (3450 16th St., 252-8711) offers herbs and massage, and is one of many alternative clinics specializing in immune system disorders.

Botanica Yoruba (998 Valencia St., 826-4967) incorporates herbal lore into an African-derived system of mysticism, healing, and charms. Here, speaking Spanish would come in handy. Votive candles and incense are as much in evidence as are plants. **San Francisco Herb Company** (250 14th St., 861-7174) has been a standby since the 1970s; it stocks teas, essential oils, spices, and extracts, and sells wholesale, sometimes.

Scarlet Sage Herb Company (1173 Valencia St., 821-0997) has bulk herbs and specializes in North American herbalism. There are fragrant gardens outside a clean shop flooded with natural light. The store's owners claim many of their herbs are organically grown or harvested from the wild.

S E C R E T
HIPPIES

San Francisco was the center of the universe — or thought it was —
during the Summer of Love in 1967, when thousands of dropouts,
runaways, and seekers flooded a working-class and student neighborhood known for cheap rents and big Victorian houses near the intersection of Haight and Ashbury streets. Later generations of dropouts,
runaways, and seekers still hang out on that corner, only now they
can take a break at Ben and Jerry's or shop at The Gap, which are
there, too.

Robin Williams jokes that people who say they can remember the
'60s weren't there, but you could do a pretty good job of convincing
yourself the '60s aren't over by spending some time in the Haight.
The half-hip, half-mean-streets stretch of Haight Street between
Masonic Avenue on the east and Stanyan Street and Golden Gate
Park on the west sports at least four — the number seems to change
with the seasons — head shops that specialize in selling incense,
rock poster art, beads, peace symbols, and other psychedelic artifacts.
The pick of the litter is **Positively Haight Street** (1400 Haight St.,
252-8747), which has just about everything a latter-day cosmic
Argonaut would want (except the still-illegal fuel). It even sells a
themed map of the neighborhood, a counterculture equivalent of
Hollywood star maps.

I lived in the Haight in the 1980s, long after the Summer of Love,
but the purple, paisley, and Day-Glo aura of those days was still very
much in evidence. I used to avoid walking past the Victorian once
inhabited by the **Grateful Dead** (710 Ashbury St.) because Deadheads
on pilgrimages would always ask me to snap their picture in front of

the house. You should probably resist the impulse to knock on the door of this private home and ask the present owner if the ghost of Jerry Garcia solos on "Dark Star" in the attic. You can also stroll past the former **Janis Joplin** residence (112 Lyon St.), or the old **Jefferson Airplane** residence (1400 Fulton St.), a big colonnaded house that the band painted black. It's now white. Or you can amble into the park and go to Hippie Hill, across the meadow from the children's playground. George Harrison went there at the height of the Beatles' fame, wearing heart-shaped, rose-colored glasses, and wasn't recognized until he took out a guitar and started playing "All You Need is Love." Wow, was he bummed out? No, man, LSD helps you to lose your ego, and, like, not get hung up on the material world and the fame game, dig?

Back in the day, people who were on bum trips for real or had physical problems went to the **Haight-Ashbury Free Clinic** (558 Clayton St., 487-5632). The clinic is still there; in fact, it's greatly expanded and internationally recognized as a leader in the treatment of drug dependencies and substance abuse. Also keeping the spirit alive, albeit in a more idiosyncratic way, is the **Red Victorian Bed, Breakfast, and Art** (1665 Haight St., 864-1978), a knowingly funky hotel with shared bathrooms that is decorated with owner Sami Sunchild's art and housed in, yes, a red Victorian.

Now that you've followed Grace Slick's directive to feed your head, you might head over to **Cha Cha Cha** (1801 Haight St., 386-5758). It has nothing whatsoever to do with the Flower Power era, having debuted in the '80s, but it's a great place. Pan-Hispanic, with Cuban pork and black beans, Spanish tapas, and incredibly good (and strong) sangria, it's a noisy, crowded, fun restaurant festooned with Santeria religious pieces and art. Be advised, Cha Cha Cha takes no reservations.

To experience a more typical Summer-of-Love-type place, leave the Haight and go to the Civic Center to eat at **Ananda Fuara** (1298 Market St., 621-1994). This is a quiet, efficient, cheap vegetarian restaurant, chiefly Indian, that serves stuff real hippies might have enjoyed in '67. It has vegetarian meats made of soy, spicy vegetable dishes, and the quintessential hippie dessert: carrot cake.

S E C R E T

ICE CREAM

For such a cool, breezy, foggy place, San Francisco's an awfully good ice cream town, with neighborhood parlors dishing out scrumptious frozen confections in down-to-earth surroundings. I attribute this to the city's insistence on authenticity, its resistance to being taken over by outside chains, and its devotion to the pleasure principle. The same passion that creates great food and wine also creates great ice cream, only the ice cream costs a lot less.

Thanks to S.F.'s Asian influence, ice cream comes in an abundance of exotic fruit flavors, as well as first-rate versions of ginger and green tea. The best green tea ice cream is made by Double Rainbow, a based-in-S.F. company that makes super-premium treats. Double Rainbow has five ice cream parlors under its own name and sells its sweet treats in many more markets and independent ice cream parlors.

My favorite place to eat Double Rainbow is the **Toy Boat** (401 Clement St., 751-7505), a combination toy store and ice cream parlor. A shelf circling the shop is lined with toys: figurines of the Simpsons, Tweetie Pie, and more. In the middle of the cheery, tidy shop is a bucking mechanical horse you can ride for a quarter. Try to get one of the booths along the back wall. The lychee nut ice cream, also by Double Rainbow, is super. **The Daily Scoop** (1401 18th St., 824-3975) also serves Double Rainbow in a laid-back Potrero Hill storefront with free newspapers scattered about.

Asian-inspired flavors are scooped at **Joe's Ice Cream** (5351 Geary Blvd., 751-1950), where Japan-born owner Mutsuhiko Murashige serves the likes of azuki bean and Thai tea, which he makes himself in a glass booth on the premises. Joe's also sells hot dogs and hamburgers, drawing moviegoers from the Alexandria Theatre across the street. The Asian flavors are the best, though there are also some traditional American flavors like bubblegum (yech!).

Fruit imported from the Philippines flavors the incredibly good desserts at **Mitchell's Ice Cream** (668 San Jose Ave., 648-2300) — baby coconut, for example, or a delectable mix of four tropical fruit flavors. It's a small place, and on a hot day in the Mission, there'll be folks licking cones out on the sidewalk. It's nearly always crowded. You take a number.

Out near the ocean in the Sunset district, where the sun rarely shines, **Polly Ann Ice Cream** (3142 Noriega St., 664-2472) sells some of the best, most unusual ice cream in the city. With more than 50 flavors — among them, licorice, red bean, and sesame — Polly Ann customers can have a hard time choosing. So the shop has a wheel of fortune on the wall. They spin it, and you agree to take the flavor the wheel picks for you. The shop also posts signs dispensing homespun advice, mostly warnings against having premarital sex. Polly Ann, which has occupied the same space on a mostly residential block since 1955, gives a free ice cream cone to dogs that trot in with their humans.

As good as it is, Polly Ann never seems to be written about. The **St. Francis Fountain and Candy Store** (2801 24th St., 826-4200), opened in 1918, is often written about, but we can't hold that against it. Go anyway. The sundaes with house-made ice cream are good and cheap, but what's really good is the place itself, virtually unchanged since the 1940s. A wooden telephone booth (with no telephone in it) recalls the days when talking on the phone was something you did in private, not behind the wheel, in a plane, or at your table in a restaurant. The St. Francis makes its own candies, including old-fashioned treats, such as nonpareils and turtles.

Since visiting Italy, I have tried in vain to find gelato as good as the stuff I had there. The closest I've come is at **Ciao Bella** (685 Harrison St., 541-4940), a hole-in-the-wall cafe practically under the Bay Bridge freeway and next door to a motorcycle shop. Ciao Bella makes its own dense, rich gelato on the premises. Its hazelnut gelato almost equals the hazelnut I had in Florence. Better yet is the coconut sorbet, sweet but not too sweet and filled with shreds of real coconut.

The most exotic flavors in the city are dished out at **Bombay Ice Creamery** (552 Valencia St., 431-1103). In a room off a bazaar where you can be fitted for a sari, or buy incense, bolts of cloth, or posters of Krishna, you can order ice cream in flavors like fig, cardamom, and the incredible saffron rose. There's a machine dispensing gumballs for a quarter, and murals of Hindu gods and goddesses on the wall, holding triple-scoop cones.

True divinity in the dessert department can be found in an authentic San Francisco treat, the oddly but somehow wonderfully named **It's It**. First made in 1928 at Playland at the Beach, a beloved and much-missed seaside amusement park, It's It survives in supermarket freezers and mom-and-pop stores. It's 340 calories of ice cream between two oatmeal cookies, dunked in dark chocolate. As you eat an It's It, you can feel your arteries congealing. It's real good.

SECRET
IRISH

As recently as the 1960s, there was an Irish neighborhood that became a gay neighborhood and was renamed the Castro. Not long before that, Irish Americans also predominated in the Mission district, which is still called the Mission but is now home to a lively mix of pan-Hispanics, dot-commers, and hipsters of all ethnicities. But while there's no Irish neighborhood within the city limits to speak of anymore, there's still a strong Irish flavor in San Francisco.

The **United Irish Cultural Center** (2700 45th Ave., 661-2700) is a popular venue for long-time favorite foods like corned beef and cabbage. It serves as a venue for Irish musicians, some visiting from the Auld Sod, and is also a place of meeting for the occasional spirited political debate. Homesick immigrants, or anyone else who wants to go to Ireland, can book a flight at **Irish Imports** (3244 Geary Blvd., 752-0961), where a travel agency shares the premises with a shop selling thick, cabled sweaters, assorted woolens, and other traditional products and novelties, such as cheeky bumper stickers. **Irish Delights** (77 West Portal Ave., 664-1250) imports claddagh jewelry, cookies, black puddings, and more. You can catch live traditional Irish music at **An Bodhran** (668 Haight St., 431-4724). Locals and visitors can keep up with the news in the *Irish Herald* (665-6653), a free monthly paper distributed in shops and bars around town.

Irish bars often serve as social centers and places to watch European football. Nearly all of them will draw you a nice pint of dark, creamy Guinness, a Harp lager, or maybe a clean, zesty Smithwick's ale. Truth to tell, though, some of the Irish bars clustered along Geary Boulevard, in the inner Richmond district, are drear, dull sports bars with bad food. However, the city has several Irish bars that rise above that lamentably low level.

My favorite Irish bar in San Francisco is **Johnny Foley's Irish House** (243 O'Farrell St., 954-0777). Foley's, run by Dublin natives, is very much like the fine Dublin pubs that serve as its model. High ceilings allow for a goodly bit of natural light. There is a long, polished wooden bar, and wood partitions to create cozy spaces — called snugs in Irish parlance. Foley's pours Guinness properly, allowing it to settle, then topping it up, and hosts visiting Irish writers for readings. It serves decent lunches — try the bread pudding made with soda bread — to modest-sized crowds, but really comes alive after work. It's loud and good-natured in the evenings, when bands play in the back room. There are DJs and dancing in the cellar on weekends.

Other good places: the **Irish Bank** (10 Mark Lane, 788-7131), a polished restaurant and bar located off an alley in the financial district, that has whiskey tastings every Tuesday from 5:30 to 7:30 p.m.; the **Dovre Club** (1498 Valencia St., 285-4169), a bare-bones drinker's bar that pulls a proper pint; and **O'Reilly's Irish Bar and Restaurant** (622 Green St., 989-6222), somewhat out of context in North Beach, which is mostly Italian. No S.F. place has been able to duplicate the best food in Ireland — the fresh trout and intensely flavorful Atlantic salmon — evidently because we're just too far away to get fresh fish from that part of the world. However, O'Reilly's does a better than credible job with Irish soda bread, made on the premises.

SECRET

ITALIAN

I'm in the classic guidebook writer's dilemma. I really want to tell you about **Laghi** (2101 Sutter St., 931-3774), because it is arguably the most distinctive Italian restaurant in a town blessed with excellent Italian food, and it doesn't get much out-of-town press. But if I tell you, and you go, my friends and I will have trouble getting a table. Oh, well. It's done now, isn't it?

Laghi is named after its chef and co-owner, Gino Laghi, who serves food inspired by his native Emilia Romagna province in Italy. The menu is small and changes often, but virtually everything here is first rate. The made-from-scratch food is robust but prepared with a light touch from the freshest ingredients. The prosciutto is house cured, the risotto is likely to show up laced with truffles and red wine, the noodles are house made. Service is unhurried but attentive; set aside some time to spend here. The wine list is mostly Italian and very well chosen; some wines come from Emilia Romagna, such as the earthy but smooth Sangiovese di Romagna. Laghi is accomplished without being precious.

Another toothsome place, located near Laghi in the Fillmore district and off the standard tourist trail, is **Vivande Porta Via** (2125 Fillmore St., 346-4430), which doubles as a cafe and deli. Delicate olive oils, spices, and cheeses line the shelves near the front of a long, fairly narrow space, while cooks in the open kitchen prepare excellent meals from the finest ingredients. Try the fettuccine alla vodka if it's on that day's menu; it's a heavenly concoction of chopped tomatoes sautéed in extra-virgin olive oil, chopped scallions, sautéed pancetta, coarse black pepper, and vodka. There are good Italian wines, many by the glass, and great desserts. Tables are small and close together, and you may have to sit at the counter, but you'll be well fed.

In North Beach, San Francisco's Little Italy (though it's not called that, just North Beach), you'll find **Gino & Carlo** (548 Green St., 421-0896). Gino & Carlo is first and foremost a bar. Most of the drinkers and bartenders know each other and don't go out of their way to please you. People are likely to be playing liar's dice at the bar, to see who will pay for the next round. On Thursdays only, Gino & Carlo hosts robust lunches, served family style at long tables, and for this the place is lively and convivial. You have to have a ticket, purchased in advance at the bar. This is an old beatnik haunt that doesn't play up its connection to the Beats. It also served as the office of the late *Chronicle* columnist Charles McCabe, who wrote his stuff in longhand at the bar and sent it to the paper by messenger.

Much of North Beach is well known — and delightful in spite of that fact. I won't dwell on places like Flor D'Italia, founded in 1886 and believed to be the oldest Italian restaurant in the country, or trendy new places like Rose Pistola, or re-born old places like Enrico's. They're good, but they don't need the attention. (For Italian coffee places that sell a bit of food, see Secret Coffee, and for pizza specialty places, see Secret Pizza.)

For a light lunch or a full dinner, **Caffe Macaroni** (124 Columbus Ave., 217-8400) is a low-key Neapolitan find. There are tables on the sidewalk, but Columbus is rife with noisy, smelly motor vehicles. Try the ground-floor cafe inside or the intimate upstairs room. Listen closely to the specials. The waiters are from Italy, and their accents are as thick as fettuccine alfredo cream sauces. The insalate pazza (watercress, strawberries, red onions, and vinaigrette) is a unique and flavorful starter, and the gnocchi is very good.

Mario's Bohemian Cigar Store Cafe (566 Columbus Ave., 362-0536) is a North Beach institution that serves house-made Campari and fabulous sandwiches on focaccia from nearby **Liguria Bakery** (1700 Stockton St., 421-3786). A small, wedge-shaped place on Washington Square, Mario's keeps a box of cigars behind the bar, but it's not a cigar store anymore. Out-of-towners wander in, but it's frequented mostly by locals.

The **Italian French Baking Co.** (1501 Grant Ave., 421-3796) is another prime place for baked goods, especially the giant sweet coconut macaroons, which you can buy with or without chocolate coating. They're a lunch in themselves. If you can find a better treat for the money anywhere, call me; I'm on my beeper.

Washington Square, across the street, is the outdoor social center of North Beach. If you get there early, you can see people from neighboring Chinatown doing their tai chi exercises. Elderly gents speaking Italian sit in the sun. On the north side of the park is the **Church of Sts. Peter and Paul**, a white Romanesque church that sees many weddings, funerals, and Catholic services. Joe DiMaggio and Marilyn Monroe had their wedding pictures taken here after being wed at City Hall: Joe with his perfectly creased suit and careful smile, Marilyn blonde and gay, while the newspapers took their pictures with big, boxy cameras and flashes.

Italian arts and culture are smartly presented at the **Museo Italo-Americano** (Fort Mason Center, Building C, 673-2200). The museum has a gallery for visual arts by Italian artists, a nice gift shop, and offers Italian language lessons. It's located in the artsy, non-profit Fort Mason Center, where most tourists don't venture. It's their loss. (For more on Fort Mason, see Secret Specialty Museums.)

Lastly, if you yearn to don the latest Italian fashions, check out **Nida** (2163 Union St., 928-4670), which features all-Italian designers. Be forewarned: you will be in tourist territory, yuppie division, on pricey Union Street, but if you shop well, you can do well at Nida and elsewhere.

SECRET
JAPANESE

Alas, there is no Japanese neighborhood anymore, due to the World War II internment that uprooted Japanese-American residents of the Fillmore district and confiscated their property. In the late 1960s, the Japan Center retail, hotel, and restaurant complex opened at Fillmore and Geary in an attempt to recreate the Japanese presence. It was only partly successful, as the random, organic charm of the old neighborhood couldn't be duplicated on demand.

That said, there are some places worth your attention in the Japan Center, where local Japanese Americans eat and shop, even though they may live far away. The **Kinokuniya Bookstore** (1581 Webster St., 567-7625) is a well-stocked place filled with books from and about Japan. Some books are in Japanese, some in English. Many titles have the fine printing and color processing that distinguishes Japanese publishing. Also in the Japan Center is **Mifune** (1737 Post St., 922-0337), a local favorite that serves cheap, basic Japanese food, especially hearty noodles. **Kabuki Springs and Spa** (1750 Geary Blvd., 922-6000) is a recently renovated place to take a steam bath and hit the cold plunge pool. And the old ways are on stage at the Japan Center every April during the **Cherry Blossom Festival** (563-2313), an annual celebration with drumming, dancing, and other performances.

Many Japanese attractions are outside the Japan Center, so you'll have to seek them out. But then, that's a good way to see the city.

Japonesque Gallery (824 Montgomery St., 391-8860) is a gift shop with the high standards and tranquil air of an upmarket art gallery. Modern, minimalist versions of traditional Japanese goods predominate, gifts are exquisitely wrapped, and Japonesque displays the advanced esthetics that you'd find in a special shop in Japan.

San Francisco has a deep talent pool when it comes to Japanese food. **Katsu** (745 Columbus Ave., 788-8050) is a low-key restaurant distinguished by its large and diverse sake menu; it pours 46 regional sakes, probably the most in the city. If you prefer your sake chilled, as I do (except in winter), try **Kabuto** (5116 Geary Blvd., 752-5652), a no-frills neighborhood spot in the Richmond. The elegant **Z Bar** in the **Hotel Nikko** (222 Mason St., 394-1111) makes sake cocktails and serves sake straight up in traditional fashion. If you're hungry, the Z Bar's bento boxes are terrific and rather eclectic. I fancy the calamari with lemon pepper aioli. The Hotel Nikko, owned by Japan Airlines, is expert in all things Japanese.

When I was introduced to Japanese food shortly after moving to San Francisco, I took to sushi right away. It was exotic, flavorful, and different, and had an edge of risk to a newcomer like me. I still like sushi, though I've broadened my palate since then. When I want first-class sushi, I go right back to Z Bar. The fish is flown in from Japan three days a week. More importantly, the sushi is made by master sushi chef Kazuhito Takahashi, who worked for the emperor of Japan. His handiwork is fresh, imaginative, expert.

Any number of pretentious sushi bars around town will bombard you with anime images on TV monitors and loud pop; their food is not the main attraction. If you want all-at-onceness and attitude, it's not hard to find.

However, if you're looking for a good neighborhood place, try **Castro Sushi** (2275 Market St., 552-2280). Look closely; it's literally underground, so you descend steps to get in. A good find in the Richmond district is **Kitaro** (5723 Geary Blvd., 386-2777). Run by a black-clad young staff, but without 'tude, Kitaro offers vegetarian sushi rolls that are actually good, as well as traditional sushi with varieties of succulent raw fish.

Japanese food is about much more than sushi, to be sure. The first time I visited Tokyo, I watched to see where office workers ate on their lunch breaks; most were heading out to inexpensive noodle shops. I followed suit. In San Francisco, I am partial to **Hotei** (1290 Ninth Ave., 753-6045), which serves big, cheap, steaming bowls of noodle soups. There's a wide range of udon (thick white flour noodles) and soba (thin buckwheat noodles) dishes. I am infatuated with the cold noodle salad with sliced cucumber at **Ten Ichi** (2235 Fillmore St., 346-3477). It's a neighborhood restaurant, very popular with locals, that has expanded in recent years but is still often crowded. Ten Ichi has a sushi bar, too — just in case.

S E C R E T
JAZZ
❀

New York it ain't, but travelers with a jazz jones can have a good time in San Francisco. Clubs, festivals, even churches burst forth with hot licks from cool players on a regular basis, and if you go out on a Monday or Tuesday night, you can hear some sounds for very little money.

A confession: the best jazz club in San Francisco isn't in San Francisco; it's in Oakland. **Yoshi's** (510 Embarcadero West, Oakland, 510-238-9200), which is both a decent Japanese restaurant, and a more-than-decent jazz club with good sound and professional management, presents national headliners in comfortable surroundings. The place has been swinging for more than 20 years and shows no signs of stopping.

Within the city limits, my two favorite places to hear jazz are within a block or so of one another in North Beach. The **Blue Bar** (501 Broadway, 981-2233) is a smoothly hip club bathed in blue light and outfitted with chairs that are, yes, blue. It has a postage stamp-sized stage and a conspiratorial underground feel — appropriately so, as the Blue Bar is located directly underneath the **Black Cat** (same contact info), a popular late-night restaurant. Although the Blue Bar doesn't match Yoshi's success in luring national names, the music is good and can range from acid jazz to a cool, smooth urban sound. Right nearby, **Pearl's** (256 Columbus Ave., 291-8255) presents local pros and visiting players who want to sit in, in warm, friendly surroundings. I saw a big band — 12 or more pieces — there one night, playing mostly for fun and in surprisingly tight fashion. On a good night, you can hear interesting improvisational stuff here.

After that trio of clubs, the regularity and quality of performances become more variable. Jazz can be heard from time to time at the **Elbo Room** (647 Valencia St., 552-7788), a venerable Mission district dive; the music room is upstairs. The **Plush Room** (940 Sutter St., 885-2800) in the **York Hotel** books cabaret pros like S.F. jazz diva Paula West, a rising star. **Enrico's** (504 Broadway, 982-6223) has Dixieland and modern jazz several nights a week. **Pier 23 Cafe** (Pier 23, the Embarcadero, 362-5125) hosts modern jazz explorers like pianist Ed Kelly. **Noe Valley Ministry** (1021 Sanchez St., 454-5238) is a Presbyterian church that hosts world music, including jazz. I've heard great shows here by Canadian American singer/songwriter Jesse Winchester and Celtic folkies, who recited Dylan Thomas's *A Child's Christmas in Wales*. The **House of Shields** (39 New Montgomery St., 392-7732), a great financial district watering hole with dark-wood paneling and an air of civilized conviviality, has live acoustic jazz after work, around 5 p.m. The band sets up next to the bar and the place fills up fast.

Beyond club dates, the jazzbeau's best bet in S.F. is to hit town during a jazz festival. The headline festival is the **San Francisco Jazz Festival** (tickets from SF Jazz Store, Three Embarcadero Center, lobby level, 398-5655), held annually since 1983. The 2000 fest, held in various venues in the fall, booked a bill that ranged from the promising Berkeley High School Jazz Ensemble to seasoned pros, such as outside piano man Cecil Taylor, song stylist Lou Rawls, bluesman Robert Cray, S.F. singer Bobby McFerrin, trumpet star Freddie Hubbard, and piano master McCoy Tyner.

A smaller, more low-key festival with a neighborhood feel is the annual summer **North Beach Jazz Festival** (267-6943, www.nbjazzfest.org). It's a week-long event with a showcase concert at Coit Tower, the landmark tower atop Telegraph Hill that reminds some people of a fire hose nozzle and others of something more intimate and male.

If you want to kick back with jazz on the radio, tune into KCSM (91.1 FM), the non-commercial campus station at the College of San Mateo, which plays a nearly all-jazz format, with some tasty blues thrown in.

S E C R E T
JEWISH

San Francisco's Jewish community is somewhat paradoxical. It's always been prominent in the life of the city, from pioneer days — when jeans-maker Levi Strauss set up a small factory, grand eccentric Joshua Norton proclaimed himself emperor, and Adolf Sutro became mayor — to recent times, when another San Francisco mayor, Dianne Feinstein, was elected to the United States Senate. There is no Jewish neighborhood in the city, however, and the physical landmarks that such a neighborhood would create are few.

That said, there are several stops largely off the tourist trail that inquisitive travelers would do well to make. One of the city's most stunning architectural achievements is **Temple Emanu-El** (2 Lake St., 751-2535), opened in 1927. You can tour this gorgeous Byzantine-Roman structure on your own. The home of a leading Reform congregation, the building yields its secrets easily to the attentive visitor. Be sure to visit the courtyard, with its fountain and mosaic trim, and the temple interior, which contains an eye-catching ark under a triangular roof. The impressive organ has 4,500 pipes.

Strauss left a legacy beyond the worldwide popularity of his jeans, originally made for prospectors in the Gold Rush. One of the city's small treasures is the **Levi Strauss Factory** (250 Valencia St., 565-9100). There are free tours of this working factory and company museum twice a week. It's all housed in a bright yellow 1906 wooden building on pretty, landscaped grounds adorned with flowers and palms.

If you can track it down, check out **A Traveling Jewish Theatre** (470 Florida St., 399-1809), which, true to its name, does travel and explores Jewish history and identity in its work. This talented ensemble company produces much original work, such as the brainy drama *Berlin, Jerusalem and the Moon*, in which a fictionalized version of the late German Jewish critic Walter Benjamin serves as the main character. Additional *gravitas* comes from **Tikkun** (575-1200), the left-liberal intellectual magazine published in San Francisco and edited by social activist Michael Lerner.

Israel's Kosher Meat Market (5621 Geary Blvd., 752-3064) is a certified-kosher deli with meat counters for chicken and red meats, two small tables inside for noshing on site, and refrigerated cases filled with red caviar, farmers' cheese, and other edibles. Israel's sells dried Manischewitz soups and Carmel Vineyards wines, and has lunch specials, such as chicken soup with matzo ball, borscht, and stuffed cabbage. Traditional bagels are made and sold at the **House of Bagels** (5030 Geary Blvd., 752-6000). While they're not quite the equals of assertive, chewy New York or Montreal bagels, these bagels are good, as are the hamentoshin cookies baked there.

In late 2003, the **Jewish Museum of San Francisco**, now closed, plans to re-open in a new location, an old brick powerhouse downtown formerly known as the Jessie Street Substation. The nexus of Jewish cultural life, the **Jewish Community Center**, is located at 3200 California Street (346-6040). Local, national, and international news of Jewish interest is tracked in the *Jewish Bulletin of Northern California* (263-7200).

S E C R E T

KIDS

Don't leave the young ones home. Bring 'em along. If they're under 11 or so, maybe they can stay in the kids-only room at the **Hotel Metropolis** (25 Mason St., 775-4600). Designed by the hotel's owner, Yvonne Lembi-Detert — herself the mother of three — the room has a Cookie Monster soap dispenser, bunk beds, and a radio pre-tuned to the Disney station. Parents stay in the adjoining room.

The city has some hidden treasures that are very much made for kids. One of the best is the **Randall Museum** (199 Museum Way, 554-9600), a really good children's museum hard by Corona Heights with its commanding view of the city and East Bay. Inside, the unassuming Randall has a petting zoo, an earthquake exhibit complete with seismograph, and art and science classes. Don't forget to go to the basement. It houses a 30-by-60-foot model train exhibit with mountains, forests, and a city and is the headquarters of the Golden Gate Model Railroad Club. On junior engineer days, kids can run the trains. The museum has no set admission. Donate what you can.

The oldest organized kid-friendly activity center in town is the wonderful **Children's Playground** (east end of Golden Gate Park). Created in 1887, it is the oldest children's playground in a public park in the United States. Swings, a merry-go-round, places to clamber and climb — they're all here, in pretty, pleasant surroundings. Directly next to the playground is the park's festive, working carousel, a true antique with gaily painted horses.

It can be tough to find kid-friendly restaurants in this city of gourmet destination dining. **Chevy's** (201 Third St., 543-8060), a bustling, upbeat branch of a chain of Mexican restaurants, is a sterling exception. Kids can run around the noisy, friendly place, no problem. And the little guys and gals are welcome to observe workers making tortillas. When my friend Deborah and her son Matthew, then age 9, visited from Toronto, Matthew was thoroughly entertained by the tortilla-making — and thrilled when he got a free dessert.

There are big-name children's clothing shops in the city, but they would be hard pressed to outdo **Tuffy's Hopscotch** (3307 Sacramento St., 440-7599). Tuffy's specializes in children's shoes with a broad range of European brands, among them Brakkies, Elefanten, and Mod'8. Socks? You want socks? They've got socks, an enormous variety of them.

Don't miss the **Basic Brown Bear Factory and Store** (444 DeHaro St., 626-0781). It's a working factory where stuffed animals are made, sewn, cut, and stuffed; kids can try their hand at some of these tasks on tours. It's kitty corner from a factory of interest to adults, the Anchor Brewing Company, where Anchor Steam Beer is made. That's beer, not bears, so kids can't go on the Anchor tours.

San Francisco led the way in interactive science museums when its now-world-famous **Exploratorium** (3601 Lyon St., 561-0360) opened in 1969. It has inspired similar hands-on science museums around the world but is still well worth a visit if you've not been. There are an estimated 600-plus interactive exhibits on hand and informed teenage guides. This place both boggles the mind and stimulates it.

The Exploratorium helped spark the creation of **Zeum** (221 Fourth St., 777-2800), a museum that emphasizes creative, feel-good self-expression rather than hard science. Kids can use personal computers to, for example, put Dad's face on his daughter's body — as a family did when I was there, to gales of guffaws — or learn how to do clay animation. They can even participate in a Web cast. The young guides explain things with the peculiar combination of languor and rapid-fire speech common in teens. My niece Kelsey had trouble swinging a golf club in an indoor game, so she expertly played a golf game on a PC. Just outside Zeum is the 1906 carousel from the now-demolished Playland at the Beach amusement park. It's heart-warming to see this vintage toy still in use and to know there's something out there for kids that's calm and not violent.

The newest mega-projects in town are Metreon, the Sony-designed entertainment and retail complex, and Pacific Bell Park, the baseball stadium for the National League's San Francisco Giants. **Metreon** (Fourth and Mission, 369-6000) is brilliantly done. Visited by six million people its first year — it opened in 1999 — it is unapologetically commercial but also boasts a fine Discovery Channel Store and a brightly interactive exhibit based on Maurice Sendak's book *Where the Wild Things Are*. If you take the kids to the movies at the center's 15-screen cinema, you may run into reporters and editors from the *Chronicle*, who sneak off to matinees. The **Long Life Noodle Company** at Metreon (369-6188) is a kid-friendly restaurant with healthful pan-Asian food. It's popular, so go there on off-peak hours; its nickname among Metreon staffers is the Long Line Noodle House. **Pacific Bell Park** (Third and King, 972-2000), which bowed in 2000, is very kid friendly and open all year. It has a free play area above the center field stands, accessible from the east side of the stadium. Best of all, there are large ground-level openings in the right field fence, so non-paying kids of all ages can catch a game for free.

Completely non-glitzy and non-commercial, **Educational Exchange** (600 35th Ave., 752-3302) is a shop even San Franciscans don't know about. It sells educational workbooks, games, maps, and toys for kids in kindergarten through ninth grade in a corner store reminiscent of a one-room schoolhouse. It is chiefly a supply shop for teachers. However, anyone can shop there. If you're home schooling a child or just want to check out the reasonably priced items, you're home.

SECRET
LESBIAN

San Francisco's lesbian community seems more home-minded than the city's gay men, but that's not to say there aren't places for gal fun and proud displays of culture.

A person could walk right by **Osento** (955 Valencia St., 282-6333) and not even know it's there, for example. It looks like a private house, but there is a women's bathhouse inside those Victorian walls. **Red Dora's Bearded Lady Women's Cafe** (485 14th St., 626-2805), an alternative-culture venue that serves vegetarian vittles, also features spoken-word performances. **Luna Sea** (2940 16th St., 863-2989) is a new performance space for works by women, including teenagers, while the **Lexington Club** (3464 19th St., 863-2052) is a bar with a reputation as a hangout for tough girls. Meanwhile, the **Coco Club** (139 Eighth St., 626-2337) has built a reputation of its own as the most stylish lesbian nightclub in town, a destination for lipstick lesbians. **Good Vibrations** (1210 Valencia St., 974-8980), S.F.'s most forward-thinking sex shop, is woman owned and lesbian friendly.

One of the city's biggest and most ambitious venues for original per formances by women is **Brava for Women in the Arts** (2789 24th St., 647-2822). Brava, which presents plays written by women of color and lesbians, is refurbishing the former York Theater, a sizable old repertory cinema, for live performances.

Sometimes the lesbian community goes public in a big way, of course. There are rich materials waiting to be mined in the beautiful **James C. Hormel Gay and Lesbian Center** in the Main Library (100 Larkin St., 557-4400). During the **San Francisco Lesbian, Gay, Bisexual, Transgender Pride Celebration Parade** held every June, there is always a starring role reserved for the motorcycle-riding Dykes on Bikes, who roar down Market Street on hot wheels.

Calendars, articles, debates, and advertisements of interest to the lesbian community are served up in **_B.A.R._** (_Bay Area Reporter_), a free weekly newspaper (861-5019). More calendars and personals see the light of day in the fortnightly _**S.F. Bay Times**_ (626-0260). Another fortnightly, _**Frontiers Newsmagazine**_ (486-6000), is a gay and lesbian-oriented freebie distributed at clubs, bars, and newsstands.

S E C R E T
L O D G I N G

Some years ago, the estimable San Francisco Convention and Visitors Bureau, which markets the city internationally and provides visitor info, dubbed San Francisco "Everyone's Favorite City." That may not be literally true, but you'll think it is when you look into the lodging situation. Since the mid-1990s, when the economy turned bullish, the hotel occupancy rate has been over 80 percent, which means few rooms are likely to be turning over at any one time, especially during

busy seasons: summer and when major conventions are in town. Room rates, too, are high, second in the U.S. only to New York. So you have to know where to look to find a great room without spending a lot.

The city's best hotel for the money is the **San Remo Hotel** (2237 Mason St., 776-8688 or 800-352-REMO), a cozy, European-style pension in a cheerful Victorian building between Fisherman's Wharf, with its bustle, and North Beach, with its Old World élan. A lot of European travelers, who are used to sharing bathrooms down the hall, stay here. The San Remo, a family-owned former rooming house lovingly restored, is immaculate, not funky. The rooms, with their big brass beds, are small and don't have TVs, if you care. Rates start at well under $100 per night. The ground-level bar and restaurant, **Emma** (673-9090), is graced with lovely stained glass and a bar shipped round Cape Horn years ago.

Of course, San Francisco has nearly all the big North American brand names and a few major Asian operators, as well. The Ritz-Carlton, Mandarin Oriental, W, refurbished Fairmont, refurbished Mark Hopkins Inter-Continental, Nikko, and many others are superb hotels, but they're not cheap. Also not cheap — but still much less expensive than luxury and high-end hotels — are properties run by S.F.'s entrepreneurial boutique hotel operators: Kimpton Hotels and Restaurant Group, Joie de Vivre Hospitality, and Personality Hotels of Union Square.

Kimpton Group founder Bill Kimpton started the boutique trend in the U.S. in the early 1980s and still runs some of the most unusual properties in town, even while expanding out of town. I like the Kimpton-owned **Vintage Court Hotel** (650 Bush St., 392-4666 or 800-654-1100), which has a California wine country theme and afternoon wine tastings in the lobby. The Vintage Court is also a rare

non-smoking full-service hotel. The **Hotel Serrano** (405 Taylor St.,
885-2500 or 877-294-9709) is also a good choice. Kimpton bought
and restored the building in 1999. The Serrano has afternoon wine
tastings in the lobby and a comfy feel.

Chip Conley's Joie de Vivre hotels have a great sense of fun and flair.
Joie de Vivre manages the **Hotel Rex** (562 Sutter St., 433-4434 or
800-433-4434), a downtown property with book-lined public spaces
and a literary theme. One of the company's pricier properties is the
20-room **Nob Hill Lambourne** (725 Pine St., 433-2287 or 800-274-
8466), which has a holistic health theme, putting vitamin pills on the
pillow instead of chocolates, and offering yoga lessons. One of its
bargain outlets is the **Phoenix Hotel** (601 Eddy St., 776-1380 or 800-
248-9466), a rock 'n' roll motel with a swimming pool in the courtyard
and a seedy Tenderloin location.

Personality Hotels opened **Hotel Metropolis** (25 Mason St., 775-
4600 or 800-553-1900) in 1999, in a meticulously restored Tenderloin
building. It gave the place a complete makeover, installing an earth,
wind, water, and fire theme. There is a soothing water wall in the
lobby, attention to feng shui principles in guest rooms, and a well-
being room for mellowing out and breathing in. The location isn't
the best, but the hotel is an oasis of calm once you're there.

Another quiet place downtown, run by Monterey's Four Sisters Inns,
is **Petite Auberge** (863 Bush St., 928-6000 or 800-365-3004). The
hotel has beveled glass French doors, French art, and a French name.
Are you getting the idea that this is a French-inspired hotel? It is, and
a gracious one, with 26 guest rooms, all with carved armoires. The
same company runs an English-style boutique hotel, the **White
Swan Inn** (845 Bush St., 775-1755 or 800-999-9570), practically next
door. There are fresh-baked free cookies by the fire in the afternoon,
teddy bears in the rooms, English art and collectibles all around. This

is too cute for some people, but others find it a great relief after a busy day.

If you're a hosteler, you can find basic, very cheap accommodations in the central city at **Youth Hostel Centrale** (116 Turk St., 346-7835) in the interesting but seedy Tenderloin. The **American Youth Hostel-Union Square** (312 Mason St., 788-5604) is a bit more comfortable, cheap though not quite as cheap, and in a less-risky location.

The aforementioned-San Francisco Convention and Visitors Bureau partners with a commercial firm, **San Francisco Reservations**, to offer hotel information, free, on the bureau's Web site at www.sfvisitor.org or toll free by phone at (888) 782-9673. The Web site has photos of guest rooms and specifics galore, as well as a rating for each hotel, assigned by San Francisco Reservations.

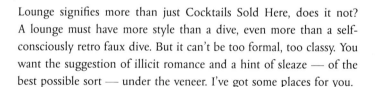

S E C R E T

LOUNGE

Lounge signifies more than just Cocktails Sold Here, does it not? A lounge must have more style than a dive, even more than a self-consciously retro faux dive. But it can't be too formal, too classy. You want the suggestion of illicit romance and a hint of sleaze — of the best possible sort — under the veneer. I've got some places for you.

Backflip in the **Phoenix Hotel** (601 Eddy St., 771-3547) qualifies. It pours bright-colored cocktails into big glasses. It's installed in a Tenderloin hotel that's got enough edge to give it a noir, slightly dangerous quality. It's got DJs playing drum and bass sounds and other stuff. It's got a pool and a blue-green hued interior. It's friendly enough, but exudes an arch attitude that lets you know that this is all a game and everyone knows it, but what the hell, why not play? Backflip is a good place to look for trouble while styling and drinking. There's a poolside happy hour on Wednesdays.

The **Red Room** in the **Commodore Hotel** (827 Sutter St., 346-7666) is another bad good bar, or good bad bar, if you will. The primary color scheme in the Red Room is — wait for it — red. The semi-circular bar is red. The bar stools, the vinyl sofas. Red, red. Like Backflip, the Red Room is installed in one of Chip Conley's theatrically designed hotels. They really are good at this thing, the Joie de Vivre people. The martinis are huge, by the way.

A very different, deliberately more traditional — not simply retro — lounge act goes on in the **Compass Rose** of the **Westin St. Francis Hotel** (335 Powell St., 774-0167). This bar, just off the lobby of one of the city's grand dame hotels and raised a bit above the lobby floor, has been around in one incarnation or another since 1904. The present version is graced by a smooth song stylist named Bob Dalpe, backed by the Rose Trio. Dalpe sings into a giant old microphone and the songs he delivers with such authority are wartime standards: 1940s tunes that could serve as a backdrop to a lovers' conversation where a woman asks, "Do you love me, Johnny?" and a man says, "Promise you'll wait for me." It's a great place for martinis, as well as champagne and caviar if you're feeling flush. There's a small dance floor and, back in the far corner, a trysting place that hotel employees call "the monkey corner" — because, as a St. Francis insider once told me, "A lot of monkeying around goes on there."

Bruno's (2389 Mission St., 648-7701) sets out the usual assortment of finger food from many lands for your grazing pleasure. But what Bruno's is really known for are its cocktails and even more specifically its cocktail crowd — and I do mean crowd, it's jammed here — busy scoping each other out. Bruno's was the hipster haunt in the mid-to late '90s, then it closed for a spell. It was revived by business partners Jon Varnedoe and Michael Hecht, the same guys who opened **Foreign Cinema** restaurant nearby (2534 Mission St., 648-7600), where patrons sip swellacious cocktails as films play on the wall. Now, Bruno's is a scene again. Go with friends to really enjoy this raucous place, thick with the sounds of jazz, rock, and a happening crowd. And look sharp. The heavy-lidded scene makers who eyeball you while you, and they, sip cosmopolitans, insist on that.

SECRET
MARKET STREET

Market Street is San Francisco's Broadway, its Champs-Elysées, its Sunset Boulevard. It's a river of humanity that begins on Twin Peaks and, like a river, winds its way downhill, picking up traffic and broadening as it goes, ending at the water: San Francisco Bay. Old-timers knew Market as the Slot and referred to the factories, warehouses, and working-class houses south of the street as "South o' the Slot." Today, the same area — transformed by hip bars, restaurants, Web-design studios, and software offices, and home to what's left of cheap housing in the city — is known as SOMA or just "South of Market."

Market Street cuts through a big slice of city life. It's a hilly residential street at its source in Twin Peaks. As it flows downhill to the Castro, it passes **Harvey Milk Plaza**, sunken below street level at

the intersection of Market and Castro and named after the martyred gay-rights leader who was assassinated in City Hall in 1978 along with Mayor George Moscone. Also near the intersection is S.F.'s great movie palace, the **Castro Theatre** (see Secret Cinema), and **Cliff's Variety** (479 Castro St., 431-5365), a neighborhood institution that really does sell variety: anything from a feather boa or a rainbow flag to a hammer or a doorknob. Burrowed away on upper Market is **Cafe du Nord** (2170 Market St., 861-5016), a hip bar with cool jazz, electronic music, hot salsa, and more in a red-upholstered space said to be a former speakeasy.

Some of the city's best places to eat flourish on or near Market. In the Civic Center at about the midpoint of Market Street's east-west run is **Zuni Cafe** (1658 Market St., 552-2522). Zuni has a happening bar in a wedge-shaped space with big windows, and a bright, talky crowd. Oysters and martinis, separately or together, star here. If you're not at the bar, try to sit in the cozy upstairs space. Way down by the bay, one block South of Market, is one of S.F.'s premier restaurants: **Boulevard** (1 Mission St., 543-6084). The restaurant is installed in a landmark 19th-century building that recalls Paris. Chef Nancy Oakes cooks superb fresh food and the place has a great wine list. At the foot of Market, in a 1916 building that was once the headquarters of the Southern Pacific Railroad, is **One Market** (1 Market St., 777-5577), a big place with big windows that serves hearty American fare. Just two blocks away is a feast for the eyes: **245 Market Street**, former home of the Matson shipping line, a vintage masonry building with huge, arched windows and a lobby decked out with marble floors and Art Deco light fixtures.

Far removed from these highlights are lowlights and lowlifes, which also abound on Market. The blocks between Fifth and Seventh streets are especially grim, rife with homeless wanderers and aggressive panhandlers, mixed in with gentle souls and outlandish characters. I call this the Fellini Promenade after the late Italian master of cinema fantasy. Operating on this stretch is the **Strand Theater** (1127 Market St., 431-1259), a former second-run movie house that now shows porn.

As I write, a new high-rise that will include a Four Seasons Hotel, retail space, and condominiums is under construction on Market between Third and Fourth streets. By the time you read this, the upscale complex may be open. If so, this block of the old street is likely to be transformed.

I don't recommend driving any downtown stretch of Market, by the way. For a variety of reasons, it is gridlocked. For instance, north-south streets usually cross Market — which runs east and west — diagonally, not directly. This crazy system helps account for the insane traffic.

SECRET
MARK TWAIN

San Francisco's journalists don't have a patron saint, but if we did have one, it would probably be Mark Twain. Twain, born Samuel Clemens, worked as a newspaper reporter for several San Francisco dailies, including the *Daily Dramatic Chronicle* (now the *Chronicle*). In the mid-1860s, young Clemens covered cops and courts, live theater, and practically everything else as the only full-time reporter on the *Call*. He was fired for what even he described as low productivity once the *Call* hired a second reporter. But before he got the axe, he became incensed when the paper's proprietor killed an article he wrote about a group of white ruffians assaulting a Chinese man on the street while a cop stood by, an attack Twain witnessed first hand.

"Usually, I didn't want to read in the morning what I had written the night before; it had come from a torpid heart," Twain recalled 40 years later in his autobiography. "But this item had come from a live one. There was fire in it, and I believed it was literature. . ." Nevertheless, it didn't run, the proprietor explained, because publishing the story would anger the white working-class readers of the paper.

Twain left San Francisco a few years later, finding fame and fortune and becoming the greatest American writer of the 19th century. He is remembered hereabouts in sometimes quixotic ways that Twain, an ironist, might appreciate. The **Hotel Mark Twain** (345 Taylor St., 673-2332), for example, is a Ramada tourist hotel with a gift shop full of S.F. kitsch like cable car fridge magnets and smiley-face buttons. The hotel coffee shop has a California Gold Rush breakfast special: pancakes or French toast, made with eggs as you like 'em. Then there's **Mark Twain Continuation High School** (1920 41st Ave.), a humble but not inappropriate honor for a writer, housed in an unadorned old building. You can also see **Mark Twain Plaza**, at the west end of Merchant Street, renamed for Twain in 1988 at the behest of poet Lawrence Ferlinghetti, who got the city to name 12 alleys and lanes for S.F. writers and artists. It is a one-block lane, not a plaza, with the Transamerica Pyramid looming at the west end and Starbucks holding down the east end. Not bad as honors go. It beats being a statue in the park christened with pigeon droppings.

S E C R E T

MURALS

San Francisco has something like 500 murals: bold street murals, accomplished murals inside major buildings, and small, homemade jobs adorning garage doors along tiny alleys.

Mexico's most famous muralist, Diego Rivera, painted several surviving S.F. works. Check out his *The Allegory of California* in the **City Club of San Francisco** (155 Sansome St., 362-2480). The piece appears in the two-story stairwell of the private club; call ahead to arrange a viewing. Rivera also painted himself painting a mural at the **San Francisco Art Institute** (800 Chestnut St., 771-7021), the city's leading art college.

Happily, good historical murals survived the transformation of the old Rincon Center Post Office into a retail and office complex. You can see artist Anton Refregier's history of northern California — for free, as with all of the city's murals — inside the renovated **Rincon Center** structure (101 Spear St., 243-0473).

More preserved works adorn the inside of **Coit Tower** (atop Telegraph Hill, 362-0808). Commissioned by FDR's New Deal in 1934, the pieces, done by a team of artists, depict Californians at work in fields, factories, and shops. Some of the murals show the faces of real people. There are also marvelous street scenes of 1930s San Francisco, painted in earth tones and populated by broad-shouldered figures. The murals were controversial because some of the artists had leftish political views. In Bernard Zakheim's *Library*, workers are shown reading socialist publications. The murals circle the tower inside on the ground floor.

New Deal-era frescoes by Lucien Labaudt depicting Californians at play brighten the ground floor Recreation and Parks visitors center at the **Beach Chalet** (1000 Great Hwy., 831-2700). The Willis Polk-designed building was used as a Veterans of Foreign Wars bar for years and in the early 1970s had one of the first Pong video games; you could barely see the murals in the murky light. The building was closed for a while, re-opening in the late '90s with a good brewpub upstairs. The murals are fully restored.

The cultural murals I mentioned earlier grow like tropical plants in the Mission, the city's predominantly Hispanic neighborhood. The area around **24th Street**, where it intersects with Bryant Street and Harrison Street, is blessed with murals. Most depict idealized Aztec figures and celebrate the Mexican heritage of neighborhood residents. The children's mini-park, located behind a wrought-iron fence on 24th near Bryant and York streets, has a profusion of outdoor murals. Best of all is **Balmy Alley**, a narrow passage between 24th and 25th streets near York, whose residents have turned practically every garage door and wall into a political and artistic statement. A slow walk down the alley reveals an eye-opening riot of color, with text in Spanish and English. "Kindness effects more than severity," one piece proclaims.

The imaginative, non-profit **Galeria de la Raza** (2857 24th St., 826-8009) is located in the heart of mural district. It has a fine gift shop, intelligently provocative window displays, and often-political artwork on display in neighboring Studio 24. The gallery is especially lively around Mexican holidays, such as the Day of the Dead (Nov. 1). A walk around the neighborhood reveals one mural after another; you're apt to get too distracted to drive.

The other prime Mission district site for murals is the **Women's Building of the Bay Area** (3543 18th St., 431-1180). The outside of this heritage stucco building is alive with swirling, vibrant murals painted by female artists and depicting women of color from many walks of life, with texts in Spanish and English. The murals, lovingly and skillfully done, wrap around the building. Look at the green columns flanking the front door; the artists have layered green paint down to the sidewalk and added roots, suggesting trees.

You can view the Mission district's murals on guided tours, complete with mural maps, through the **Precita Eyes Mural Arts Center** (2981 24th St., 285-2287).

Those are highlights but, really, murals abound all over town, not just in the mural zones.

If you ride, or you're in the neighborhood, check out the **Duboce bicycle mural** (Duboce between Market and Church) on the back of the Safeway supermarket. This is an imaginative, environmentally themed, block-long painting, done by artist Mona Caron.

Or walk up Broadway just east of Columbus Avenue in North Beach, turning at Romolo Place, the little lane that runs up to Fresno Alley. There you'll see a mural called *Gold Mountain*, painted in 1994. You'll have to look past the graffiti added by someone unlikely to become the next Keith Haring to see the piece, which depicts the history and struggles of Chinese Americans in California. It's worth the effort.

SECRET
MUSEUMS

The Big Five major museums each have their quirks, peculiarities, and areas of specialization. It's the quirks, as well as their strong core holdings, that make these institutions interesting.

Take the **California Academy of Sciences** (Music Concourse, Golden Gate Park, 750-7145), as an example. A marvelous natural history museum with a planetarium and an aquarium, the Academy also has a Far Side Gallery that displays 150 original drawings by the science-minded *Far Side* cartoonist Gary Larsen. Once you've seen the sharks and the sea urchins in the Steinhart Aquarium, you can wander into the Larsen gallery to figure out just what he meant by the cartoon about cow tools. The Morrison Planetarium puts on star shows that still seem pretty wondrous, even in this age of interplanetary space probes. And for a really creepy experience, visit the Insect Room.

The **San Francisco Museum of Modern Art** (151 Third St., 357-4000) is known for cutting-edge visual arts, mounting major exhibits of works by video artists like Bill Viola, as well as accomplished painters like Magritte. Museum director David Ross, who championed video art in the 1970s and ran New York's Whitney Museum, likes to push the limits. SFMOMA is probably just as well known for its form as its content, being housed in a 1995 building by Swiss architect Mario Botta with a 145-foot-high skylight atrium and striped exterior. It has become something of a cruising scene for singles on half-price night, which is Thursday. The museum has also won a youthful audience with private, late-night showings organized by the artists' group Blasthaus. Maybe you can get in. Look for event listings online at www.sfmoma.org or www.blasthaus.com.

The **California Palace of the Legion of Honor** (34th Ave. and Clement, 863-3330) has a strong collection of Rodin sculptures and holdings of Impressionist and other European paintings. That figures, since the lovely hilltop building, opened in 1924, was inspired by the Hotel de Salm in Paris. Even so, the Legion, beautifully renovated in the late 1990s, is just as notable for its Egyptian art and other antiquities. Do look in on its collection of porcelain. And don't miss the Achenbach Foundation collection of prints and drawings; there are some 75,000 pieces, displayed through frequently changing exhibits. Walking up to the Legion is almost as good as being inside. Rodin's *The Thinker* shares the courtyard with a small glass pyramid that recalls I.M. Pei's big glass pyramid at the Louvre. Paris, again.

The **M.H. de Young Memorial Museum** (Music Concourse, Golden Gate Park, 863-3330) is, like the Legion, a city-owned museum. The de Young has been in the park for a century and is S.F.'s oldest art museum. It is particularly strong in American art, with paintings by James Whistler, Georgia O'Keefe, Grant Wood, and many others, and artisan work by Paul Revere, the Boston silversmith who took the famous midnight ride. California artists like Wayne Thiebaud are also well represented. The de Young is closed for major renovation until 2005.

Some art critics regard the **Asian Art Museum** (Music Concourse, Golden Gate Park, 379-8800) as the most important museum for Asian art and antiquities outside Asia. Chicago industrialist and former Olympic Games president Avery Brundage donated his vast collection to the city in 1966, jumpstarting the museum, which has added to its core collection since then. The museum's holdings go back 4,000 years and include sculpture, ceramics, metalwork, jewelry, painting, and calligraphy. In 2003, the Asian will move to a new location, the renovated Old Main Library, in a major makeover led by architect Gae Aulenti, who converted Paris's old Orsay train station into the sparkling Musée d'Orsay.

To save money on your museum-going, buy a **City Pass**, which offers a 50-percent discount on admissions to the major museums (except the Asian), as well as the Exploratorium and other sites. It's on sale at the Visitor Information Center in Hallidie Plaza.

Also, if your hunger for art is matched by a hunger for good food, you can dine well in the cafes at major museums. Especially notable are the **Legion Cafe** (221-2233) at the Palace of the Legion of Honor, and **Caffe Museo** (357-4500) at SFMOMA; the latter has delicious modern Italian food, good coffees, and very drinkable wines by the glass.

(See Secret Specialty Museums for more museum info.)

S E C R E T

MUSIC STORES

Chary of chains, San Franciscans love all things independent, so it comes as no surprise in this alternative-minded town that some of the best music stores are quirky, individualized operations. Add that to the best of the chains — Virgin and Tower — and you have a deep supply of good sounds.

Bird & Beckett Books & Records (2788 Diamond St., 586-3733) is a small, fiercely independent operation that stocks a large number of vinyl records for purists who complain that compact discs just don't get it done. The stock includes an interesting selection of used jazz and classical records. The Classical Annex at **Tower Records** (2568 Jones St., 441-4880) is another good place to look for classical recordings.

For rock music, **Amoeba Music** (1855 Haight St., 831-1200) is hard to beat. Spread out in a cavernous space that used to house Rock & Bowl, a bowling alley that played music videos, Amoeba is true to its name. It keeps changing shape, offering vinyl here, CDs there, rock poster art, fanzines, world beat here, salsa there, headbanger metal way over there. **Aquarius Records** (1055 Valencia St., 647-2272), by contrast, is a hole in the wall on the hip strip of Valencia, and is very focused on altie-rock and local bands. **Open Mind Music** (342 Divisadero St., 621-2244) is a local favorite, also long on vinyl, back issues, and used sides; you'll see patrons with headsets and turntables checking out the merchandise. **Record Finder** (258 Noe St., 431-4443), as its name suggests, supplies hard-to-find stuff. **101** (513 Green St., 392-6368) is a small place with a big collection of vinyl and musical keepsakes, such as Sgt. Pepper's Lonely Hearts Club Band lunchboxes.

Many San Franciscans won't admit it, but they shop the chains, too. The big **Tower Records** store (Columbus at Bay, 885-0500) is a barn-like place and a long-time favorite. The **Virgin Megastore** (2 Stockton St., 397-4525) is a new favorite, with a voluminous selection of rock, country, jazz, blues, world beat, and almost everything else. If you decide you've listened to enough music and want to make some, hie thee directly to **Lark in the Morning** (The Cannery, 2801 Leavenworth St., 922-HARP). Don't be put off by the slightly cute name; this is a terrific store for musical instruments, especially traditional ones: bells, lutes, bagpipes, mandolins, whistles, and harps. And the shop is serene without being cult-like creepy. I think it's because the people in it are doing something they really like.

SECRET
NEWSSTANDS

San Franciscans hooked on newsprint are still mourning the loss of Harold's, a venerable international newsstand that went to the big recycler in the sky in 2000. We'll just have to get over it, get on with our lives, and meet our publication needs at these other very fine places of business.

Juicy News (2453 Fillmore St., 441-3051) is a newsstand with a juice bar. That's right: if the reading isn't juicy enough for you, there's always orange and mango in a cup. **Cafe de la Presse** (352 Grant Ave., 398-2680) is a stylish and popular cafe strong on international magazines and newspapers that has much more élan — and food, good food, which Harold's never had. This is the place to look for *Paris Match, Stern*, the *Independent on Sunday*, and Italian *Vogue*, and have a coffee. **City Lights Bookstore** (261 Columbus Ave., 362-8193) is more than a great bookstore; it's a great newsstand, with political and literary mags from around the country and the world, many with an anarchist or otherwise leftie bent. Another good bookstore with an incredible newsstand is the **Booksmith** (1644 Haight St., 863-8688), which stocks more than 1,000 periodicals.

Other good places to pursue your passion for pulp are the independent video stores, nearly all of which have newsstands and often stock a lot of zines. Some of said zines obsess about video and film, and others about practically anything. Therefore, you should not neglect **Le Video** (1239 Ninth Ave., 566-3606), the City Lights of cinema, which has an extensive selection of film periodicals. For tattoo magazines, zines, and comix, try **Leather Tongue Video** (714 Valencia St., 552-2900), **Naked Eye News & Video** (533 Haight St., 864-2985), and **Aquarius Records** (1055 Valencia St., 647-2272).

Other good sources: **Smoke Signals** (2223 Polk St., 292-6025), which has a very good and wide-ranging stock of international fare, including periodicals in Arabic, Japanese, German, and Italian. Run by Beirut-born Fadi Berbery, the shop has wall clocks showing the hour in times zones around the world. **Fog City News** (455 Market

St., 543-7400) is a little downtown place that also brings in international stuff for your global reading pleasure.

SECRET

NICHE BOOKSTORES

In college football, they publish polls listing the Top 20 teams. I'm going to do that here with niche bookstores. There's certainly enough of them, and they're good enough to have their own Top 20. Here it is, in no particular order.

The puzzle over where to find a fine mystery bookstore has been solved: it's the aptly named **San Francisco Mystery Bookstore** (4175 24th St., 282-7444), which has practically every sleuth story and whodunit tale between covers, both new and used. The mystery of where to find an incredible cookbook is over, too: it's surely at the culinary supply store **Sur La Table** (77 Maiden Lane, 732-7900), which stocks more than 700 cookbook titles. There is another strong cookbook section at **Rizzoli** (117 Post St., 984-0225). It's also a good place to find books from Italy, as well as literature and art books. And, as always with Rizzoli, the store is beautiful.

If it's travel and geography you're interested in, go to **Rand McNally** (595 Market St., 777-3131), a spacious corner store stuffed with travel guidebooks, with a great sampling of globes in the window. For more incredible globes — globes with topographic surfaces, globes that illuminate, globes with historical patterns and themes — try **Thomas Brothers Maps** (550 Jackson St., 981-7250), which is owned by Rand McNally and located in the Jackson Square Historic

District among lovely old brick buildings. Thomas Brothers is one of my favorite shops; I could get lost in there for hours. And speaking of getting lost, you can find travel books galore at **Get Lost Travel Books** (1825 Market St., 437-0529), which stocks city and country maps, language tapes, atlases, and travel gear.

But suppose it's architecture and design you want to read about. No problem. **Richard Hilkert Bookseller** (333 Hayes St., 863-3339) has a great line of titles about interior design, as well as belles lettres and music; it stocks mostly new books, along with some out-of-print titles. **William K. Stout Architectural Books** (804 Montgomery St., 391-6757) is the prime destination in town for intelligent and often beautiful books about architecture. **William K. Stout Design Books** (27A South Park, 495-6757) offers a counterpart to the architecture books, concentrating on books about interiors and design. It's situated in a white-brick building with a cool, quiet feel in Multimedia Gulch, where software design is the usual topic. If you find yourself in Ghirardelli Square and tire of the knickknack shops, pop into **Builders Booksource** (900 North Point St., 440-5773), where you can pick up books that will show you how to fix just about anything.

San Francisco is rightly known for its social conscience and embrace of diversity. Logically, then, the city is home to a major bookstore for books about, and often by, gay men and lesbians: **A Different Light** (489 Castro St., 431-0891). S.F.'s ethnic diversity has also produced notable foreign-language bookstores. **La Casa del Libro** (973 Valencia St., 285-1145) specializes in Spanish books. **Mariuccia Iaconi Book Imports** (970 Tennessee St., 821-1216) sells Spanish, Italian, and English-language titles. Books about Japan, some in Japanese and some in English, are on hand at **Kinokuniya Bookstore** (1581 Webster St., 567-7625) in Japan Center. **European Book Company** (925 Larkin St., 474-0626) has volumes in a variety of languages, including bilingual dictionaries. **Marcus Books** (1712 Fillmore St., 346-4222) has books on African American themes, usually written by African American authors, and is one of S.F.'s venerable independent bookstores. **China Books and Periodicals** (2929 24th St., 282-2994) operates out of a small storefront in the inner Mission. In the 1970s, before there was much of an exchange of people and ideas between America and the country most Americans still called Red China, this was an important bookstore, a rare source of books from and about China. They're not so rare anymore, but China Books is an especially good source for Chinese children's books in English and translations of Chinese literature.

Sometimes, older is better. If you're in search of antiquarian books, rare books, and out-of-print books, try **Tall Stories** (2141 Mission St., 255-1915). You press a buzzer on the street level to enter the building, climb the stairs . . . and, behold, lots of great, musty volumes. **W. Graham Arader** III (435 Jackson St., 788-5115) is as elegant as its name. Situated in a vintage Jackson Square building, it specializes in rare books, maps, and prints.

If you're counting, that's 19. But I'm counting the William Stout architecture and design stores as one entity, so it's really 18. There are two to go, and they are beauties. Not as specialized as the others, they're just good independent booksellers.

A Clean, Well-Lighted Place for Books (601 Van Ness Ave., 441-6670) is exactly what its name promises. It has a great selection, a surprising mix of genres, and a helpful and knowledgeable staff who will gladly order books for you. Locally owned Clean, Well-Lighted also has an ambitious and active authors' reading program, mixing talented local authors and touring celebrities. In a one-month period in 2000, the store hosted Amy Bloom, T.C. Boyle, Armistead Maupin, Ursula LeGuin, Elmore Leonard, and David Leavitt.

The Booksmith (1644 Haight St., 863-8688) is a neighborhood bookshop with a citywide reputation. The staff is super, always there to help out, and they care about books. The store has an excellent periodical rack — actually, two periodical racks — and is a stop for touring authors.

In the mid-'90s, I wrote an article for the *Examiner* about science-fiction author Harlan Ellison writing a short story at a desk in the Booksmith's front window. Ellison arrived not knowing what he was going to write about. By arrangement, Robin Williams came by and gave him a one-line premise; it was something about computers and had the word byte in it. "You rat-fink!" Ellison exclaimed in mock horror. "You know I don't have a computer." Ellison was the good soldier, though. He worked on the story all day in the Booksmith's window, as people milled around and walked by outside, thinking, "What the hell?" It was eventually published somewhere.

SECRET
NOT OF THIS EARTH

Simply walking around San Francisco, there are times when you just don't know where you are. Not just what street you're on, but what planet you're on. It's that kind of town.

Case in point: one of the most interesting San Franciscans, a chap well known to the locals, who see him everywhere, is the 12 Galaxies Man. Nicely dressed, he's in early middle age, I'd guess. He's always wearing sunglasses, often mysterioso mirrored jobs. Spend any amount

of time here and you'll see him, too. He shows up everywhere, striding purposefully down the sidewalk carrying a sign that reads, "Impeach Clinton. 12 Galaxies. Guiltied to a Technitronic Rocket Society." Huh? you think. Whaddya mean 12 galaxies? What does Technitronic mean? And what does Bill have to do with it? Lucid answers are not forthcoming. I've no idea if we are in one of the designated 12 galaxies right now. No idea what the end of Clinton's presidency means to the 12 Galaxies Man. His concerns are clearly Not of This Earth.

Nor are many of the concerns addressed in the rarified books at **Field's Book Store** (1419 Polk St., 673-2027), which specializes in metaphysical titles. Nothing Technitronic, as far as I know. But Aleister Crowley, Madame Blavatsky, astrologers of many lands, adepts on various planes of existence, and masters of the occult do live on in the pages of books sold here. The **Psychic Eye Bookshop** (301 Fell St., 863-9997) sells similar stuff, but more than books is available: you can have a psychic reading done seven days a week or have your astrological chart done in just an hour. Hey, this is the 21st century; cosmic doesn't have to mean eternal. Walk in or make an appointment. They know you're multi-tasking and time challenged.

Those who have departed this earth dwell in customized urns at the **San Francisco Columbarium** (1 Loraine Ct., 752-7891). In an 1898 sort-of-Roman-looking circular building with a 75-foot-high domed rotunda are the ashes of several thousand former Earthlings. The facility, which is splendidly designed and has been carefully maintained by the Neptune Society since 1980, is beautiful to the eye, if a little eerie.

Eeriness gives way to something verging on horror when you stand frozen like a deer caught in the headlights while Laughing Sal towers over you, raising storms of mechanical laughter at your predicament. Laughing Sal is the prime exhibit at the **Musée Mecanique** (1090

Point Lobos Ave., 386-1170), an eccentrically engaging, paint-peeling, decrepit, admission-free venue for old games and novelties that held sway before the birth of video games. Some are 100 years old, and some are naughty: peep shows from before 1910. Laughing Sal, who looks like Clarabelle's evil twin, is a clown figure in a display case that emits horrible laughter when you drop a coin in the slot. Sal is, I think, supposed to be female, but you just don't know. She was a star at Playland at the Beach, a seaside amusement park demolished in the early 1970s, and appeared in the Orson Welles film *The Lady from Shanghai.*

SECRET OUTLETS

Clothes by the pound, discounts on big-name clothing brands, food for cheap — they're all available.

The clothes by the pound place is **Clothes Contact** (473 Valencia St., 621-3212), where you literally buy used, vintage, sometimes once-worn women's clothes by weight — $8 a pound when this book went to press. Clothes Contact's German-born owner imports many items from Germany, where ladies run to large sizes, so this store is a boon for big girls looking for coats, hats, dresses, the lot. Prices aren't as low, but the discounted clothes are new, at the **Esprit Factory Outlet Store** (499 Illinois St., 957-2540). The place has a high-tech, high-ceilinged look with display racks on wheels.

For food at low, low prices, try the **Bargain Bank** (1541 Polk St., 345-1623 and 599 Clement St., 221-4852), an outlet for soft drinks, candy, beer, wine, and canned goods, often sold at less than half the normal retail price. Another good place to go for discounted groceries is the **Grocery Outlet** (1717 Harrison St., 552-9680). I found drinkable zinfandel here for $4 a bottle, good merlot for $5. Huge cartons of canned food, cereal, and household goods in the warehouse-like space are a bargain-hunter's cornucopia.

SECRET
PARKING

I don't suppose "Abandon Hope All Ye Who Enter Here and Plan to Park" would be a good slogan for the city. And, indeed, it's not strictly true that parking is hopeless; it just seems that way. There are more people and more vehicles every year, but not more streets or more parking spaces. In fact, due to building construction and infrastructure upgrades, there are actually fewer parking spaces now than there were just a few years back. In this environment, if you're looking for street parking, you'll have to get lucky. Ordinarily, the way to find street parking is to be the first to spot a car that's leaving and get over there. Otherwise, it's off to the lots and garages, which are usually crowded and overpriced.

Still, there are a few possibilities. If you're downtown and going to Metreon, the San Francisco Museum of Modern Art, the Yerba Buena Center for the Arts, or the stores, the major garage is the city-owned **Fifth and Mission garage** (Fifth and Mission). This seven-story garage has been known to fill up by noon on a weekday, earlier on a

Saturday. Your best bet is to head directly to the top floor. Most people drive fruitlessly round and round on the lower levels in hopes of avoiding the open-air rooftop. Let them. Save time by heading to the place where you have the best chance of finding a space. In North Beach, where finding parking is — hard to believe — even tougher, your best bet is the **Vallejo Street garage**, right next to the Central Police Station. People apparently think a sign on the garage that says "Police Parking" means the whole garage is for the police, which it isn't. Again, go to the open-air rooftop. The weirdly slanted roof, which looks like it was designed by or for Doctor Caligari, is usually open, and has a splendid view of the cityscape.

On the street, it's really tough. For downtown parking, go to **Harrison Street**, between Fourth and Fifth streets, near the big Office Depot building. There's sometimes parking there, especially on weekends. Best of all: no meters.

Unless you don't care about parking tickets — or worse, the tow truck — don't emulate the locals, who fecklessly park in the center turn lane on the busy **Valencia Street** nightclub corridor, thus making horrible traffic even worse. Instead, try the public lot on 21st Street east of Valencia, which isn't outlandishly expensive and has an attendant. I don't recommend doing as the Romans — er, San Franciscans — do by parking on the sidewalk. It blocks ease of movement for a lot of people and will not endear you to the neighborhood or the police one little bit.

The best way to get around the central core, if you're able bodied and the weather is fine, is by walking. The horrible parking is matched by horrible driving conditions, but the city is compact, and many places of interest to visitors are surprisingly close to one another. You'll see more on foot. And you'll get your circulation moving.

S E C R E T
PARKS

In this town, Golden Gate Park is the mother of all parks, but it is far from the only one. Often-overlooked Lincoln Park is a gem, and the Presidio is a former U.S. Army post that is now part of the Golden Gate National Recreation Area's 74,000-acre domain. Along with lovely vest-pocket parks like Alta Plaza Park and Lafayette Park, they are the city's lungs and its alternately restful or exhilarating green spaces.

Golden Gate Park (Ocean Beach to Stanyon, Lincoln to Fulton) is three miles long and a half mile wide. Within its 1,017 acres are massively, and deservedly, popular attractions and low-key retreats. Among the former are the park's fine museums (see Secret Museums) and the wonderful **Children's Playground** (see Secret Kids), both at the eastern end of the park. Another popular attraction toward the eastern end is **Strybing Arboretum and Botanical Gardens** (661-5191), which includes native California plants endangered in the wild, rare magnolias that blossom nowhere else, and the 18,000-volume **Helen Crocker Russell Library of Horticulture**. The crowded but fun **Japanese Tea Garden** (752-1171) is also located at the eastern end. It includes a steeply arched footbridge you practically have to climb; big, beautiful goldfish; and a tea and cookies pavilion where a Japanese-American entrepreneur introduced the fortune cookie. Everything is free, aside from the museums and the tea garden, which is free the first Wednesday of the month.

Some parts of Golden Gate Park are frankly old fashioned, and often all the more enjoyable for not trying to be trendy. At **Stow Lake**

(752-0347), you can rent canoes or pedal-boats, or surreys with fringes on top for land transport, which also move by foot power. Climbing Strawberry Hill on the island in the lake rewards you with a panoramic city view, where trees do not block it. The little snack shop at Stow Lake sells Eskimo Pies, ice cream sandwiches, and the S.F. ice cream treat It's It, plus popcorn for people or waterfowl. "Ducks like popcorn" reads a sign in the shop. Similarly old fashioned are the radio-controlled model boats on Spreckels Lake in the western reaches of the park, and the fly-casting at an angler's pond nearby. Ditto the bowling green, where you can get **free lawn bowling lessons** (681-1580 or 864-1843). You wear flat-bottomed shoes for this relaxing retro activity.

Additionally, there are footpaths galore throughout the park, with paths near the museums and Music Concourse rife with plants, not people. If you've always wanted to be a man on horseback (or a woman in the saddle), check out the **Golden Gate Park Stables** (668-7360). Bicycle rental shops are bunched along Stanyan Street (see Secret Bicycles).

The Presidio (561-4323, northern waterfront, just south of the Golden Gate Bridge) is even bigger than Golden Gate Park. The Presidio's 1,480 acres contain countless trees, a bowling alley, an 18-hole golf course, 11 miles of hiking trails, 14 miles of trails for cycling, and the headquarters of non-profit organizations in some of its 500 historic buildings. The former Army post also includes a pet cemetery popular with fans of bizzaro kitsch. Crissy Field, along the park's northern waterfront edge, is a prime place to run dogs (see Secret Dog Friendly). The Presidio is still being developed as a park, since it joined the Golden Gate National Recreation Area only in 1994. A 12-page brochure for self-guided walking tours is available free at the **William Penn Mott Jr. Visitors Center**.

Big, impressive parks like the Presidio and Golden Gate Park are joined by small, restful greenswards around town known primarily to neighborhood residents. **Lafayette Square** (between Gough, Laguna, Sacramento, and Washington) is one of the best. A small, square park with a woody knoll in the center, it has a few amenities like water fountains and restrooms. But it is chiefly good for strolling, playing Frisbee or walking to Washington Street at the top of Pacific Heights to gaze at the bay below. The exquisite two-story private residence at **2151 Sacramento Street** was briefly the home of Sherlock Holmes creator Arthur Conan Doyle, and bears a small plaque. The plaque doesn't mention this, but the house was also the home of Albert Abrams, a medical doctor who took a bizarre turn into fringe medicine, claiming he could cure nearly anything with electronic gizmos. Before Abrams died in 1924, the American Medical Association called him "the dean of 20th-century charlatans." **Alta Plaza Park** (between Clay, Jackson, Steiner, and Scott) is another neighborhood gem. Terraced with incredibly steep concrete steps and topped by ancient tennis courts and a few trees, it can seem almost vertical and startlingly dream-like, like something from out of an Antonioni film. **Dolores Park** (between Dolores, Church, 18th, and 20th) is a sunny, hilly park in the Mission district with palm trees and places to laze on the grass. Local residents have had trouble with drug dealing and pit bulls in parts of this park over the years, but there has been improvement of late. The southwest corner, where people sun themselves, is known to locals as Dolores Beach.

Lincoln Park (between Clement, 33rd, and the ocean) includes two popular attractions: an 18-hole golf course and the **California Palace of the Legion of Honor** (see Secret Museums). But the park has secrets, too. Just off Clement at the top of the hill is a horse corral for park rangers' mounts and a cluster of picnic tables and grills that are nearly always available. On quiet days, neighborhood residents can hear the animals whinnying, not a common sound in any city. Just past the stables are virtually unknown concrete bunkers dug in under yards of rock that were built for protection against a feared Japanese invasion in World War II. Now used for storage, they are off limits inside and have an eerie, end-of-the-world quality viewed from the outside. At **Fort Miley**, a federal post that rubs shoulders with Lincoln Park, are picnic tables commanding stunning views of the ocean behind the Veterans Administration Hospital. A few yards from the tables is a hillside footpath dedicated to veterans of the Battle of the Bulge. You'll see more orange California poppies than people on this path above the Pacific.

SECRET
PERIODICALS

It's a literate and opinionated little big city we have here, with many and diverse periodicals. So finding out what is going on, where, and when is usually a snap.

The dominant publication for news, entertainment, food and wine writing, and sports is the daily ***Chronicle***. For arts and entertainment coverage, look for the *Chronicle*'s Datebook section. Datebook is the name of both the daily entertainment section and a tabloid stuffed into the big, break-your-back Sunday *Chronicle*. The Sunday Datebook features voluminous listings and feature stories on pink paper: thus, its nickname, the Pink Section. The daily *Chron* is the best source in town for reviews, with the city's best critics and columnists. Much of the print publication's content appears on-line at sfgate.com.

The city's second, much smaller, daily is the *Examiner* (www.examiner.com). S.F.'s Fang family has acquired the *Examiner* name and some physical assets — but not the staff, which merged with the *Chronicle*'s when the *Ex*'s old owner, the Hearst Corp., bought the *Chron* in late 2000. The Fangs publish Chinese newspapers and a thrice-weekly giveaway, the *Independent*. Their *Examiner*, of course, has news, listings, and reviews, as the undistinguished *Independent* does, but the paper's long-term scope and quality aren't yet known.

The two major alternative weeklies are familiar versions of papers in many North American cities: free tabloids stuffed with personals, classified ads, and calendars heavy on alternative-flavored arts and entertainment. Reporting and reviewing in both the older, larger *Bay Guardian* (www.sfbg.com) and the younger, semi-large *S.F. Weekly* (www.sfweekly.com) are very uneven, sometimes sharp and insightful, sometimes given over to therapeutic self-expression. Politically, the *Bay Guardian*, aimed mostly at readers under 35, is the creature of its sixtysomething owner, founder, publisher, editor, and offensive coordinator, Bruce Brugmann, who gives his paper a bellicose, conspiracy-minded tone. The *S.F. Weekly*, owned by an Arizona-based corporation but published in San Francisco, is contrarian, taking the attitude that you're probably too stupid to understand what it's about to tell you one last time, and is aimed at twentysomethings. Both papers publish good listings, which are by far the most read parts of the weeklies. The best alternative weekly, with the sharpest writing and thinking, is the Berkeley-based *Express*, lightly distributed in S.F.

San Francisco, the monthly city magazine, is a fairly representative example of the genre. A handsome publication with color photography and slick paper, it targets chiefly upscale professionals. *San*

Francisco's mainstays are trend-spotting pieces, celebrity profiles, and the occasional piece of investigative reporting. The magazine has good listings and capsule reviews of restaurants and attractions.

The city has a plentitude of niche periodicals published for, and usually by, specific audiences. The **B.A.R.** (*Bay Area Reporter*) is a gay weekly and the **S.F. Bay Times** is a gay biweekly; both report on timely issues in the gay community and publish extensive listings. Chinese-language periodicals, often localized editions of Hong Kong papers, are widely available in the Chinese community, and the Fang family's **AsianWeek** is a nicely designed national tabloid based in S.F. **El Tecolote** is a socially conscious, bilingual monthly newspaper published in Spanish and English and edited by Juan Gonzales, who founded the paper in 1970. The **Jewish Bulletin** is a professionally edited monthly newspaper long on news and opinion pieces.

Some of the city's more interesting papers are neighborhood sheets, worth picking up if you're in the 'hood. The **Potrero View** is a feisty tabloid published on Potrero Hill since 1970. **New Mission News** is a tough-minded, crusading monthly published since 1980 in the Mission district. The quarterly **North Beach Now** is a deft blend of old and new in the city's traditional entertainment center and Euro-flavored neighborhood. These papers avoid slickness in favor of a sense of engagement and first-hand familiarity.

Still other publications target communities of interest. Among them: *SF* **Arts Monthly** (www.sfArts.com), a freebie with features and schedules of gallery shows and performances, distributed at arts venues and downtown locations, and *SOMA*, which covers South of Market arts and scene-making.

San Francisco is a world center of technology magazine publishing, infusing said periodicals with dot-com sensibilities and New Economy data and buzz. Titles like **Wired**, the first widely successful international new-technology magazine, **Red Herring**, **Upside**, **Business 2.0**, and **Smart Business** reflect the city but don't cover it as such. The same goes for prime online enterprises, such as CBS **MarketWatch** (www. marketwatch.com), an investment site founded by former *Examiner* executive editor Larry Kramer; **CNet** (www.CNet.com), a technology site and cable TV venture; and **Salon** (www.salon.com), an arts, politics, and cultural site launched in 1995 by former *Examiner* editors and writers. S.F.'s activist side shapes *Mother Jones*, the country's largest left-liberal magazine, published since 1976.

S E C R E T

PHOTOGRAPHY

I know. It's good to find great places with awesome views and photograph them. Or to find places with great ambience and photograph them: maybe an artfully blurry look for the action shots, grainy B&W for the moody stuff. But viewing photography by great photographers is fun, too. Does Ansel Adams sound good? How about Robert Frank or Dorothea Lange?

The major institution with a continuing commitment to photography, and the budget to act on its commitment, is the **San Francisco Museum of Modern Art** (151 Third St., 357-4000). SFMOMA has a department of photography and commandeers its third-floor gallery for changing exhibitions. Also notable for fine photography is the nonprofit gallery SF **Camerawork** (1246 Folsom St., 863-1001), installed in a space South of Market. Camerawork specializes in new work with an edge and has a small bookstore. The **Ansel Adams Center**

(495-7000), operated by the Friends of Photography, is named in honor of the San Francisco native son who won fame for his breath-taking, silvery nature shots. As this book went to press, the Ansel Adams Center was relocating from its gallery on Fourth Street to a new space at 655 Mission Street near SFMOMA and the Yerba Buena Center for the Arts. The monthly magazine *Photo Metro* (243-9917) publishes photographic art and tracks the scene.

The private **Fraenkel Gallery** (49 Geary St., 981-2661) and private **Robert Koch Gallery** (49 Geary St., 421-0122) often display new photography. Both galleries are located in a downtown building near the intersection of Geary and Market streets that is something of a hive for art galleries.

Definitely the most interesting proto-photography in town can be found at the **Camera Obscura** (1090 Point Lobos Ave., 750-0415), located behind the Cliff House on a concrete deck at the bottom of cracked concrete stairs. It shares this weird little corner of S.F. with the Musée Mecanique and Laughing Sal, resident seagulls, the guano-coated rocks offshore, and the breakers rolling in off the ocean. The camera obscura, a device used by Leonardo de Vinci, con-sists of a building with a darkened interior, a big lens, and a curved, parabolic screen onto which images of the area outside are projected. There's something fascinating about it. You see people walking around and birds wheeling by in a way that seems almost magical and a little sneaky: you see them but they don't see you or know you're watching. The 1949 building is shaped like a big camera. It's dingy around the edges. Inside it also has small holograms; maybe the owners didn't think the camera obscura would hold people's attention. It held Ansel Adams's attention, though. The late photog-rapher used to drop by here often, go inside, and peer at the living shoreline.

SECRET
PIZZA

You can find really good pizza in the most unlikely places. The half dozen or so restaurants I gravitate to for their pizza are found all over town, including in the Mission (mostly Hispanic) and in the Richmond (mostly Asian and Russian). Only one truly outstanding pizza place is located in North Beach, the city's traditionally Italian neighborhood.

That single exception, however, happens to be really good. **Tommaso's** (1042 Kearny St., 398-9696) has been a local favorite for generations. Opened in 1935, it was the first place in town to make pizzas in a wood-fired oven. Tommaso's is Neapolitan, so it serves savory, thin-crusted pies with traditional toppings: mozzarella, tomato sauce, pepperoni, garlic. You enter the small, dark interior by carefully feeling your way down three stairs from the street, where you line up with other famished diners; Tommaso's doesn't take reservations. It's family owned and seating is family style at long tables. When I was there last, I arrived soon after opening to find the staff in the booth reserved for family and in the midst of a card game. When the orders were taken, the servers went back to cards. Yet, they were never less than perfectly attentive and efficient.

Small, individual-sized pizzettas are the best items on the menu at **Mescolanza** (2221 Clement St., 668-2221), though it's a full-service restaurant serving northern Italian fare. Thin-crusted, fragrant, full of flavor instead of undercooked dough, Mescolanza's pizzas are almost cracker-like and nearly greaseless. Try a pizzetta funghi (mozzarella, mushrooms, tomato sauce), insalata mista with great house dressing, and a bottle of Machiavelli Chianti Classico; the label carries the likeness of this cynical student of human nature.

Only a block away is **Pizzetta 211** (211 23rd Ave., 379-9880), which also serves thin-crust, individual-sized pizzas with delicious toppings. Installed in a tiny former bakery, the restaurant makes more room in fine weather by setting out sidewalk tables on a usually quiet street. The roasted eggplant, portobello mushroom, goat cheese, and basil pizzetta is delicious, and the house scores with its cheese board of American farmhouse cheeses and French plums.

The lightest, finest pizza in town may well be at **Pauline's** (260 Valencia St., 552-2050). Located in a canary-yellow wooden building next to the Levi Strauss Factory and Museum, Pauline's puts egg whites in its crusts, which are almost ethereal. The pesto pizza may not be to die for but it could well be worth killing someone else for (I'm kidding!). Incredibly good Louisiana andouille sausage, a good selection of vegetable toppings, and a great selection of beer that includes Sierra Nevada Pale Ale and Haacke-Beck, the best alcohol-free beer, round out the menu.

For something completely different, check out **Zante Pizza and Indian Food** (3083 16th St., 621-4189), which marries curry and other spices from the subcontinent with pizza. And for crusty, chewy, old-fashioned Italian pizza dripping with cheese and sauce that runs down your chin, you could do a lot worse than **Gaspare Pizza House** (5546 Geary Blvd., 387-5025). Red and white checked tablecloths add a traditional touch, and the green vinyl booths all come with wall-mounted jukeboxes. The house wine is dubbed spaghetti red.

For convenience, **North Beach Pizza** (five locations) is popular mainly for keeping late hours. **Extreme Pizza** (four locations) is popular mainly for having an of-the-moment name.

SECRET
PORN

Once upon a time — it was the 1970s, actually — San Francisco was, along with New York and Los Angeles, a place where many, many smutty movies were made, and a place where they were shown. Adult movie theaters, most of them former legit houses that had seen better days — much better — and sleazy, smelly peepshows were all over the central city. Production shifted south to L.A. and video killed most of the theaters, but video stores persist — at least until the Internet kills them.

Locals and visitors in search of raunch-o-rama can still find it, even if the screens got smaller. Looking for the new issue of *Wanker's World* magazine? Try the shops on the sleaze strips along Broadway near Kearny Street; Market Street between Sixth and Seventh streets; and Folsom Street between Fifth and Eighth streets. For nasty videos — say, *Video Vixxxens Vol. 233* — the same places apply, along with the following.

Frontlyne Video (1259 Polk St., 931-9999) has a small selection of mainstream movies but is chiefly a pornography emporium. Most rentals go for $2, which is probably the cheapest rate for any kind of movie in town. **North Beach Video & Movie** (1034 Kearny St., 391-1073) specializes in, uh, special tastes. It sells — not rents — porn movies at astronomical prices ($50 to $100 each) for videotaped activities that are sometimes indescribable and often inexplicable. **Le Video** (1231 and 1239 Ninth Ave., 566-3606), the city's best source for legit — that is, foreign, classic, independent, and Hollywood movies — also maintains a porn department on the second floor of

its store at 1239 Ninth Avenue. In the store at 1231 Ninth Avenue, Le Video has a rack of vintage 16mm films transferred to video for rental. A series called Bucky Beaver has great liner notes written by an understandably anonymous scribe. "A hippie-type guy with scraggly hair and pimples gets it on with a young blonde who's way too cute for him," reads one set of notes.

There are very few adult theaters left that show hardcore movies. The most visible example, because it's on a busy downtown street, is the **Strand Theater** (1127 Market St., 431-1259). Sadly, this was a discount repertory cinema until recently but gave up and went to porn. Another is the **Adult Mini Theater** (Golden Gate and Jones, no listed phone), in the dankest, seediest part of the Tenderloin. I have to admit, courage failed me when it came to paying $5 and walking into this place, which reportedly projects old hardcore movies on a wall. It's one of the very few venues of any kind cited in this book that I didn't visit first hand. You're on your own with this one.

SECRET
PUBLIC TRANSPORT

Alert visitors will quickly notice that San Francisco does not have an efficient and extensive public transport system to rival, say, those in New York, London, Tokyo, or Hong Kong. That said, there are virtues to the public transport system here. First, it is cheap by world standards; the Municipal Railway, which runs city buses, light-rail Muni Metro trains, and the famous cable cars, charges just $1 for buses and rail, and transfers are free. (The cable cars are $2.) Second, there is a dazzling array of choices: buses, light rail, cable cars, subway trains, regular surface rail, and ferries. And third, the cross-section of people and great variety of views you get on public transit can't be matched in the encapsulated environment of a private car — although walking will certainly do the same thing, and San Francisco's compact central city is a fine place to walk for the able bodied.

The **Municipal Railway** (673-6864), known to San Franciscans as **Muni**, is the agency that locals love to hate. Budget cuts, cushy union rules that allow drivers to skip work a certain number of days without even calling in, dirty vehicles, safety problems, and more plagued Muni in the 1980s and 1990s. By the late '90s, city coffers overflowing with cash and the concentrated heat of public wrath made city officials pay attention. Muni is not world class, but it has improved.

To save even more money on the cheap fares, buy a one-, three-, or seven-day "passport" at the Visitors Center in Hallidie Plaza. They're good for any Muni vehicle. If you're here for at least a couple of weeks, get a Fast Pass, sold in various locations, including some retail outlets. If you're paying Muni's basic $1 fare, you must have exact change. Cable cars — they're not called trolleys, since they run on metal cables and don't have engines — will make change.

If you're interested in lively and scenic rides, check out the **F streetcar line** that runs down Market Street, along the newly spiffed-up Embarcadero all the way to Fisherman's Wharf, a five-mile trek. The streetcars, which date from the 1930s and '40s, have been meticulously restored, with new paint jobs. This line was launched in 2000, and it's brilliant.

For a funkier experience, take the **14 Mission bus**, which goes through working-class and hipster zones along Mission Street. The **30 Stockton bus** winds slowly through North Beach and Chinatown, past Union Square shopping, and across Market Street to Metreon, the Moscone Convention Center, and the Caltrain rail commuter station. The **22 Fillmore bus** goes through the Marina district along the gentrified northern waterfront, climbs the vertigo-inducing Fillmore Street hill in Pacific Heights, and rolls down Fillmore through funkier environs in the Western Addition and on into the Mission.

Bay Area Rapid Transit (650-992-2278), known by its initials as BART, was long derided for tardiness and equipment failures. The regional light-rail service has improved in recent years; except for the occasional suicide diving onto the tracks or faulty equipment, BART is reliable. With gleaming metal cars, usually clean inside, it is also a pleasant way to ride. Your Muni Fast Pass is good on BART in the city. In 2003, BART will open a station at San Francisco International Airport, providing a much-needed service.

AC **Transit** (510-817-1717) runs buses between S.F. and Oakland, Berkeley, and the East Bay. It used to be superb, with interesting drivers. One guy, who drove the 2:13 a.m. F bus, the last bus leaving S.F. for Berkeley, used to softly play a jazz radio station, burn incense stuck onto the fare box and, rather alarmingly, drive his night shift in sunglasses. AC Transit doesn't have as much panache now. The incense man is gone, as is much of the system's budget.

The most civilized way to travel is surely on the water. **Golden Gate Transit** (455-2000), which also runs cushy, clean buses between S.F. and Marin County at the northern end of the Golden Gate Bridge, operates fast, fun ferries between S.F. and Sausalito. The ride takes about 25 minutes. It's bracing and breezy out on San Francisco Bay. And it's often chilly; zip up. **Blue & Gold Fleet** (773-1188) runs a network of ferries between the city and destinations such as Alcatraz, the hiking and historical mecca of Angel Island (the West Coast version of Ellis Island for Asian immigrants), and Sausalito. The

Alameda-Oakland Ferry (510-839-2882) operates pleasant commuter ferries between the city and the East Bay.

If you're going down the Peninsula toward Silicon Valley, Stanford University, and environs, **Caltrain** (800-660-4287) runs hourly commuter trains between San Francisco (Fourth and Townsend) and downtown San Jose. The trains are comfortable and clean and move at a steady pace, though they will never be mistaken for bullet trains. **Samtrans** (also 800-660-4287) runs an efficient bus service between downtown S.F. and San Mateo County on the Peninsula.

SECRET
RADIO

San Francisco and Bay Area radio is amoeba-like, always changing shape. There are more than 70 FM and AM radio stations in the immediate area, broadcasting in a bewildering welter of formats, with diverse and often-clashing sensibilities. Most struggle to be heard over the hilly terrain. Niche programming rules here, as everywhere, in an era of focus groups, corporate consultants, and bottom-line mentalities. In this sea of call letters, a few islands of innovation and relative sanity breach the surface.

San Francisco pioneered American freeform underground rock radio in the 1960s at FM stations KMPX and KSAN. Although it was erratic and could be wildly undisciplined, freeform radio initiated the use of album tracks and often worked socially conscious commentary into the format. Echoes of that era can be heard on **KFOG** (104.5 FM), a superior Baby Boomer station that mixes new tracks, rock classics, local bands, and occasional live concerts. Its "gray-haired ponytail moment" musical flashbacks are evocative and funny, and "Acoustic Sunrise" on Sunday mornings is engagingly eclectic. Old-time KSAN stalwart Scoop Nisker, who wove collages of music and news, shows up on KFOG with an occasional commentary. The present KSAN (107.7 FM) plays headbanger rock and classic guitar bands, and has the city's most talented drive-time DJ in John Grapone. KITS (105 FM), which calls itself "Live 105," is home to new rock sounds: "Subsonic," which airs from midnight to 4 a.m. Sunday mornings, plays techno. KLLC (97.3 FM), which calls itself "Alice," is a vehicle for young female artists, such as Alanis Morissette, Fiona Apple, and Jewel, and has a sterling nighttime DJ in Sterling James, who brings wicked sharp humor to her show. Hip-hop rules the airwaves on KMEL (106 FM) and KWLD (94.9 FM).

The AM giants are KGO (810 AM), which has scored the area's top ratings for more than 20 years with a live-wire mix of news and talk, and KCBS (740 AM), which maintains numerous Bay Area news bureaus but hamstrings its reporters with a rigid news/traffic/weather format designed for dial-pushers with short attention spans.

For edgy, indie, alternative rock, the best bets are college and non-commercial FM stations on the leftward end of the dial: KUSF (90.3 FM), the campus station at the University of San Francisco; KALX (90.7 FM), out of the University of California at Berkeley; and KPOO (89.5 FM). The POO in KPOO's call letters stands for "poor"; the station was launched in the 1970s as "poor people's radio." It maintains a community focus, with blues, reggae, rock, and rap music mixed with commentary and public affairs.

For years, the Bay Area jived and jumped to the sounds of KJAZ, an all-jazz station whose programming was also carried in Japan. When KJAZ went silent, it was a perilous time for jazz fans. But KCSM (97.7 FM), the campus station at the College of San Mateo, has proven to be a capable successor, albeit with a relatively weak signal. KCSM broadcasts an eclectic jazz menu, mixing national jazz commentators like Stanley Crouch with welcome dollops of blues music.

On the classical front, **KDFC** (102.1 FM and 1220 AM) is the bearer of the torch. It is a fairly conservative station, sticking mainly to chestnuts, with chatty DJs who mix biographical anecdotes about singers and composers with the music. The station's Web site, kdfc.com, is a good source of information about upcoming classical music events.

The major public affairs stations are National Public Radio affiliates KQED and KALW. **KQED** (88.5 FM) airs NPR programming and strong local news produced under news director Raul Ramirez. KQED's weekday morning talk show "Forum," hosted by San Francisco State University English professor Michael Krasny, is the city's smartest general-interest talk show. **KALW** (91.7 FM) is smaller than KQED but has more soul. KALW ranges widely for programming, supplementing local and NPR material with the Canadian Broadcasting Corporation's "Sunday Morning" and "As It Happens." KALW may have the area's best arts and cultural program host in Alan Farley.

To the political left of NPR stations is **KPFA** (94.1 FM), a Berkeley-based station with a strong, 50,000-watt signal. Founded in 1949 as the first non-commercial, listener-sponsored station in the United States, KPFA started as a libertarian, free-speech station. It morphed in the late 1960s into a New Left activist outlet, and morphed again in the 1970s and beyond, becoming a bastion of tedious identity politics. In the late 1990s, management's heavy-handed efforts to provide much-needed updating sparked a staff strike that nearly silenced KPFA. It survives and is an outlet for talented radio veterans like talk-show host and correspondent Larry Bensky. The anti-KPFA is **KSJO** (740 AM), a shout-radio vehicle for political rants from the right.

SECRET
REVOLUTION

San Francisco sometimes seems quite apart from the rest of the United States, a fantasy island of liberalism and radicalism in a conservative country. A haven for freethinkers since the 19th century, the city was a hotbed of antiwar activism in the Vietnam War era and has since served as an incubator for environmentalism, modern feminism, and gay and lesbian activism. In the 1980s, when Ronald Reagan mesmerized America, Jessie Jackson carried San Francisco in the Democratic Party primary election.

The city honors its working-class heritage with detailed, well-written historical markers on the Embarcadero near Market Street that recall the General Strike of 1934, when the National Guard killed two workers on strike for decent wages in Depression-era America. The Art Deco beauty of the **Sailors Union of the Pacific** building (450 Harrison St.) is a reminder of the age before ship containerization, when S.F. was one of the busiest ports on the West Coast. The round, modern **Longshoremen's Hall** (400 North Point St.) is another physical reminder of union activism; the hall is often used as an entertainment venue.

Present-tense activism survives, however, nowhere more so than at the unprepossessing, walk-up offices of **Global Exchange** (2017 Mission St., 255-7296). Global Exchange leads drives for non-exploitative fair trade and against sweatshop conditions in the Third World. The non-profit organization is serious minded, committed, and always looking for volunteers. It leads "reality tours" to various Third World countries (including parts of the United States) with a meet-the-people theme. Global Exchange runs the **Fair Trade Craft**

Center (4018 24th St., 648-8068), where you can find handicrafts made by artisans that Global Exchange contracts with directly. Look for the big purple awning out front.

One of the city's best bookshops is **Modern Times** (888 Valencia St., 282-9246), a non-sectarian bookstore well stocked with left and radical political writing, fiction, and non-fiction from Third World countries. There's also a pleasant children's book room topped by a brightening skylight. Politics, cultural studies, and literature predominate in this first-rate bookstore. **Bolerium Books** (2141 Mission St., 863-6353) in the Mission district specializes in labor history, ethnic studies, and African American issues. These bookshops double as de facto information centers and bulletin boards for upcoming political events.

Several key Web sites also serve as digital Paul Reveres for the long-pending second American Revolution. Among them are the Web site of the *San Francisco Bay Guardian* newspaper (www.sfbg.com), the political site **ProtestNet** (www.protest.net), **Global Exchange**'s site (www.globalexchange.org), and the popular **Craig's List** site (www.craigslist.org.)

S E C R E T
ROCK 'N' ROLL

San Francisco rocks. It has since the 1960s, when the city spawned bands like the Beau Brummels, then went crazy in the psychedelic era with Jefferson Airplane, Big Brother and the Holding Company, Quicksilver Messenger Service, Country Joe and the Fish, and, of course, the Grateful Dead. Since then, Carlos Santana and Chris Isaak have had good rides on the charts, as have acts like Journey and Huey Lewis and the News. S.F. is not a big production center, like L.A., but musicians like to live here — it's creative enough, yet removed from most of the pressures and temptations of the business. Van Morrison, Bonnie Raitt, Neil Young, and other luminaries have made homes in or near the city.

To catch live rock, the 11th Street corridor between Folsom and Harrison streets is the best place to go. The headliner club here is **Slim's** (333 11th St., 552-0333), owned by the smooth soul crooner Boz Scaggs and specializing in rootsy rock, rockified country, and blues. On the same block is the **Paradise Lounge** (1501 Folsom St., 861-6906), a barebones place with three stages. The Above Paradise room is set aside for acoustic stuff and spoken-word performances. Unsigned bands and touring acts stop by.

Bottom of the Hill (1233 17th St., 621-4455) has the obligatory pool tables, a patio for smokers who need to feed their habit, passable food, and a stage that holds some of the hippest bands going. This is probably the prime venue in town for cutting-edge bands. **Justice League** (628 Divisadero St., 289-2038) is another place to hear punky, cutting-edge bands, although DJs have made major inroads here, so it's also a dance club and often filled with recorded music. **Hotel Utah** (500 Fourth St., 546-6300) is a venerable music venue in a funky Victorian building; the club leans toward rootsy, folkie stuff and is a comfortable spot with a small stage and second-level viewing gallery. The **Great American Music Hall** (859 O'Farrell St., 885-0750) has the city's most inclusive, high-quality popular music: rock bands, folkies, singer-songwriters, world music and ethnic acts, as well as jazz groups. The GAMH is in a former bordello decked out in red rococo style, with columns and a horseshoe-shaped balcony; the balcony is the best place from which to see the stage.

Touring headliners come calling at the **Warfield** (982 Market St., 775-7722), a one-time theater converted into a big, noisy, happening club. The original San Francisco rock emporium, the **Fillmore** (1805 Geary Blvd., 346-6000), was the launching pad for psychedelic bands in the Flower Power era, when the late Bill Graham was S.F.'s powerhouse rock promoter. The Fillmore is huge, and a good place to wander around between or before sets. There's a bar on the first floor and two more bars upstairs at the balcony. Don't forget to read the decor. Framed rock posters grace the walls, as do reprinted newspaper articles from the late Ralph J. Gleason, a powerful *Chronicle* and *Rolling Stone* music critic who championed San Francisco bands, and Jann Wenner, from back in the days when *Rolling Stone*'s founder reviewed shows for the *Daily Californian*, the student paper at UC-Berkeley.

SECRET
RUSSIAN AND
EAST EUROPEAN

He steps outside, goes down the stairs, turns left. He walks past the bakery, skirts the newsstand overflowing with newspapers, goes by the video store, the bookstore, the delicatessen, and into the pharmacy. He makes a purchase, taking care not to snare his cassock as he opens the door, and throws back his long, gray ponytail, which he wears in a single braid. Satisfied all is well, he heads back up the hill, nodding hello to the woman at the register in the gift shop. He opens the tall golden door and goes back to work.

The man is a priest at **Holy Virgin Cathedral**, a big, gold-onion-domed church of the Russian Orthodox Church Outside Russia (6210 Geary Blvd., 221-3255). I often see him making his rounds in the Russian colony along Geary, especially in the densely concentrated strip between 15th and 25th avenues. He ministers to the Russian-speaking community in the cathedral with its four tall golden doors and mosaics facing Geary. Maybe he teaches at the cathedral's Orthodox school, Saint John's of San Francisco Orthodox Academy.

The Holy Virgin Cathedral is the spiritual center of a significant Russian community that increased its numbers in San Francisco soon after the 1917 Bolshevik Revolution, then again in the 1980s when an exodus of Soviet Jews left for new lives in the West. Today, the community is well established, keeping one foot in the American mainstream and one foot in Russian culture. Many of its children attend public high schools, where they learn English. But people who choose to do so can live day in and day out in the Richmond district speaking Russian, eating Russian food, watching Russian movies on video, reading Russian books and periodicals, worshipping in Russian churches.

One of the most intriguing Russian places — located outside the Geary corridor — is **Archangel Bookstore** (1352 Ninth Ave., 242-9698), which advertises itself as the home of "mystical and patristic books." It's a fascinating store. A sign posted on the door offers classes with a Russian master in making Orthodox icons. Sacred music plays on the sound system. Incense burns. Icons keep watch from the walls and shelves. Books in Russian and English exploring the mystical traditions of Eastern Christianity are on sale.

Most Russian businesses are less esoteric, concerned with earthly matters. If feeding your stomach takes priority over feeding your soul, **Gastronom** (5801 Geary Blvd., 387-4211) is a must. This bright corner deli brims with smoked fish, piroshki, a variety of spirits (among them, Ararat, an Armenian brandy), dense, chewy Russian and German black and rye bread, black and red caviar, trays of smoked fish, and three varieties of mushroom salad. They make fresh-cut sandwiches, too, although ordering one is a challenge for patrons who don't speak Russian, as there is no English menu and the ladies behind the counter aren't fluent in English. Just smile and point.

Heaps and heaps of Russian breads can be found in the **Moscow and Tbilisi Bakery** (5540 Geary Blvd., 668-6959). And cakes, busily decorated and lathered in cream. And strudels, with cherries or poppy seeds, sold for under a dollar even though they're bigger than a boxer's fist. And meat and cheese blintzes. In the corner is a community bulletin board, along with a stack of copies of the Russian-language biweekly newspaper *24 Hours International.*

Several Russian pharmacies offering free delivery operate along the Geary corridor, as do nearly bare storefronts used for shipping packages. Of more interest to visitors are **Torgsyn** (5542 Geary Blvd., 752-5546), which buys and sells estate jewelry and antiques, and **Troika** (5050 Geary Blvd., 387-4345), which sells fine blue and white porcelain, framed paintings, some jewelry, and the famous Russian egg-shaped dolls within dolls. **Regina** (5845 Geary Blvd., 386-8577) sells icons, glittery rings, and old Russian and Soviet military ribbons. **Bouquet** (5815 Geary Blvd., 751-2222) is an aptly named Russian-run flower shop. Right next door to Bouquet is **Continental Video** (5813 Geary Blvd., no listed phone), which augments earnings from Russian videos by renting mailboxes, which take up one wall.

Polish businesses pop up here and there, too. **Seakor** (5957 Geary Blvd., 387-8660) is a Polish deli and sausage factory that turns out intensely flavorful kielbasa and garlic sausages, and makes fresh sandwiches. A broad selection of Polish, Russian, Armenian, and other ethnic favorites is available at **European Food** (3038 Clement St.,

750-0504), which has terrific imported cheeses, silvery and golden smoked fish, yogurt, beer, bread, and a deli counter with salmon, herring, and cabbage salad. For dessert, there is halvah and many creamy cakes. European Food sells many items wholesale.

Eastern European restaurants are not numerous hereabouts, but several places are worth checking out. **Russian Renaissance Restaurant** (5241 Geary Blvd., 752-8558) has a tent-like awning over the entrance to its mustard-yellow and black building, and serves heavy but savory Russian cuisine. A better choice from a gastronomic standpoint is **Old Krakow** (385 West Portal Ave., 564-4848), a Sunset district Polish restaurant with original art on the wall and well-prepared versions of traditional Polish food on the table — not too heavy, yet unstinting in the flavor department. The hearty soups are especially good.

S E C R E T
SAILING

When a city has water on three sides, said city has plenty of opportunities for sailing and boating. You can do the sailing yourself by renting a boat for a day, or you can kick back and let others do the sailing for you. However you do it, get out on the water. The most beautiful views of the city are from the ocean and the bay.

Pacific Marine Yachts (50 Francisco St., 788-9100 or 800-2-YACHTS) has three yachts for rent that can handle small or large groups, and offers a Sunday champagne brunch aboard its 150-foot *San Francisco Spirit* that will definitely put you in a celebratory mood. You can also rent boats and spend the night aboard one at **Pier 38**

Maritime Recreation Center (Pier 38, the Embarcadero, 975-3838). For more adventurous outings on the Pacific, try the **Oceanic Society cruises** (Fort Mason Center, Building E, 474-3385) to the offshore Farralon Islands; you can see whales, puffins, and sea lions from the non-profit society's 63-foot vessel. Another non-profit outfit, **Sailing Education Adventures** (Fort Mason Center, Building E, 775-8779), offers sailing lessons for children and adults, as well as environmentally themed lectures and field trips.

Spinnaker Sailing (Pier 40, the Embarcadero, 543-7333) has boats from 20 to 80 feet for rent. If you want an updated Bay Area-wide listing of what boats are available at any given moment, contact **Comesailing.com San Francisco** (1650 Sacramento St., 673-5562 or www.comesailing.com).

For really low-key boating, head over to the **Stow Lake Boathouse** in **Golden Gate Park** (752-0347). For a nominal fee, you can rent a rowboat or pedal-boat and cruise around this pleasant manmade lake, sharing the right of way with ducks and seagulls. It's incredibly relaxing. Buy a bag of popcorn and take it with you. The ducks will love you for it.

SECRET

SAM SPADE AND DASHIELL HAMMETT

Dashiell Hammett, a Pinkerton detective who went on to create the shrewd fictional shamus Sam Spade, left his mark on San Francisco's literary landscape. Hammett lived in the city in the early 1920s and set crime novels and short stories in S.F. in the late '20s and '30s, moving on to Hollywood and eventual blacklisting in the McCarthy era for his left-wing politics. A surprisingly large number of the places Hammett wrote about — or worked and lived in — have survived the wrecker's ball, albeit with dramatically varying degrees of style.

If you take a Sam Spade/Dashiell Hammett walkabout, you'll find out soon enough why detectives were called gumshoes. The path will take you down some of the toughest, grimiest streets in town, as well as into some of the most elegant office buildings and a classy restaurant.

Hammett lived at **620 Eddy Street**, in an apartment building that still stands. It's caged with bars on windows and doors now, to keep out the crack addicts that infest this strip of the Tenderloin. The building is directly across the street from the **Phoenix Hotel**, a hipster's hangout whose bar, Backflip, is a favorite for cocktails and latter-day lounge lizards. The tough surroundings give youthful urbanites a frisson of fear; it makes them feel alive. The day I walked by 620 Eddy, hired muscle dressed all in black and wearing headsets were shepherding the hoi polloi on the sidewalk at the Phoenix for a special promotional event — no connection to Hammett. As for Sam Spade, Hammett had him living not far off at **891 Post Street**, another tattered, scarred Tenderloin locale. Even in the daytime — a walk at night is inadvisable — street people howl at invisible demons. This is Hell on the half shell.

Matters improve considerably in downtown locations associated with Hammett's work. Just off Bush Street near Stockton is **Dashiell Hammett Street**, renamed for the writer at poet Lawrence Ferlinghetti's behest. It's a steep, one-block lane lined with handsome, well-tended apartments. Not 100 yards away on the other side of Bush is **Burrit Street**, a dingy alley marked with a wall plaque that reads "On approximately this spot, Miles Archer, partner of Sam Spade, was done in by Brigid O'Shaughnessy," a reference to Hammett's *The Maltese Falcon*. Look up; the plaque is above your head on the battleship-gray wall of an old apartment building.

Appropriately, Burrit is a dead-end. Just a few doors down, above the Stockton Street Tunnel, is a bar called the **Tunnel Top** (601 Bush St., 982-2307). Here and there the bar's windows are broken; where they're not broken, they wear a coat of grime that's been there since Brigid snuffed Miles. Directly across the street, at **608 Bush Street**, is another literary site: Robert Louis Stevenson boarded there in early 1880.

Sam Spade's mythical office was located at 111 Sutter Street, in a very real and very beautiful office building. Constructed in 1926, the **Hunter-Dullin Building** has a relief of Mercury outside, green marble in the lobby, and Mayan iconography above the main entrance.

By now, you've probably worked up an appetite. If so, stop in at **John's Grill** (63 Ellis St., 986-0069). Sam liked to eat there, dining on chops, baked potatoes, and sliced tomatoes, a combination John's will be happy to serve you. Photos of old-time San Francisco line the dark-paneled walls, and an atmosphere of elegance prevails. Try the Oysters Wellington and have a drink in memory of poor Miles and the no-good dame who did him in.

SECRET
SCIENCE FICTION

Fantasy writing, speculative fiction, sci-fi, science fiction: call it what you will, it's probably in stock in a good specialized bookstore or video shop around town. (See Secret Video.) All of those interrelated genres are in ample supply at **Borderlands Books** (534 Laguna St., 558-8978), which specializes in used and new science fiction, fantasy, and horror titles. In classic independent bookstore fashion, Borderlands supplies overstuffed armchairs for patrons and never hustles you out of them just to make a sale. The store also has an active and high-quality authors' reading series. **Elsewhere Books** (260 Judah St., 661-2535) is a small but good source for science fiction, horror, and mystery writing. **Tall Stories** (2141 Mission St., 255-1915) has a well-stocked selection of science fiction and mystery titles, and sells first editions. **Fantasy Etc.** (808 Larkin St., 441-7617) specializes in new and used science fiction, rounding out its offerings with detective fiction and a great, appropriately musty-smelling line of old pulp magazines; some go for prices geared toward collectors rather than browsers. For affordable stuff, bargains can often be had in used bookstores, so see Secret Used Books for more on that.

S E C R E T

SENIORS

The magic word is discounts. Some 500 San Francisco businesses offer discounts to older travelers. Some discounts start at age 65, although quite a few kick in as early as age 60. The best way for seniors to get broad information about San Francisco is to call the **Senior Information and Referral 24-Hour Line** at 626-1033. It's not a voice-mail system but a telephone line manned by city employees, usually from the **Commission on Aging** (25 Van Ness Ave., Suite 650, 864-6051). Be sure to ask for the *Senior Gold Card Merchant Discount Directory*, a printed listing of some 500 S.F. businesses that give discounts to seniors, typically ranging from five to 20 percent off standard prices. San Francisco's city government does not publicize this program outside the city limits and operates it chiefly for residents. But the fact is that the directory is available to anyone who knows to ask for it, and the discounts listed are available to any senior, from anywhere, who asks for them and has proof of age. **Moose's** (1652 Stockton St., 989-7800), a see-and-be-seen power restaurant on Washington Square, knocks 15 percent off the bill for seniors Sundays through Thursdays. The *U.S.S. Pampanito* (Pier 45, Fisherman's Wharf, 775-1943), a restored World War II submarine, waives admission fees for seniors. The **Roxie Cinema** (3117 16th St., 863-1087), an adventurous repertory movie house, takes more than half off for viewers over 65, who get in for three bucks. There's lots more: pharmacies, restaurants, airlines, golf courses, dentists, doctors, acupuncturists, museums, tours, and others slash prices for older people. Some clerks don't know about the discounts or don't mention them on their own. Ask and ye shall receive.

San Francisco's hills can be a problem for anyone with limited mobility, but motorized transport definitely helps. If you are 65 or older, you can ride the **Muni** (Municipal Railroad) buses and streetcars for just 35 cents instead of the usual $1. Cable car fares drop from $2 to $1. Happy trails!

S E C R E T
SEX CLUBS

Poet George Sterling called San Francisco "the cool, gray city of love." It is that, especially on a foggy evening, when the romance of the city's maritime climate and port of call history can be achingly intense. But San Francisco is simultaneously the hot young thang's lust connection. Sometimes sex in the city is amazingly structured and specific. For example, **Eros** (2051 Market St., 864-3767) is a sex club that caters exclusively to gay men, and not all gay men but gay men from ages 18 to 29. The club features a European steam room, backroom maze, sauna and video lounge, and, uh, playrooms. Eros is spread out over two stories and makes a point of promoting safe sex. There is a mixed gay and straight clientele at the **Power Exchange** (74 Otis St., 487-9944), which bills itself as a "sex multiplex for the wickedly adventurous." Here, too, there is more than one floor, and a plentitude of toys and special situation rooms, such as an interrogation room, for acting out sexual fantasies. The Power Exchange also emphasizes safe sex, but pretty much anything goes at this kink-o-rama provided it is consensual. At vsf (278 11th St., 621-4863), a South of Market nightclub, there is primarily a heterosexual scene, heavy on the latex outfits and known chiefly for Bondage-A-Go-Go parties on Wednesday nights. Whaddya mean, let you up?

SFO

⚜

The facts on the ground at the end of the day — as they say in pundit-speak — are these: **San Francisco International Airport** (650-761-0800, www.flysfo.com) is fifth nationally and ninth internationally in passengers carried, with more than 40 million. SFO, as it is known, has but two runways to handle all the flights for those 40 million-plus people. The runways are only 750 feet apart because they were designed in the 1930s for smallish aircraft. In fine weather, no problem. But because they are close together, authorities shut down one (or both) runways in inclement weather, with fog and wind being the usual culprits. That means, in addition to the statistics just cited, there is one more stat of note: SFO is the worst airport in the United States most years for delayed departures and arrivals.

Given that you may spend a lot of time at SFO, by far the Bay Area's biggest and busiest airport, what can you do there? If you have access to the first-class or business lounges, good for you. If you don't, there are still interesting things to do. In fact, you may want to leave the lounge to shop, snack, or hit the museums.

That's right, museums. SFO's **Airport Museum** is the only academically accredited museum in the world located in an airport. All three terminals — North Terminal, South Terminal, and the stunning new International Terminal, which opened in late 2000 — display clever exhibits in clear glass cases located in high-traffic public areas. Exhibits are keyed to popular culture. Items like martini mixers, old radios, lunchboxes, or football memorabilia, carefully arrayed and accompanied by informative texts, are located in galleries throughout the airport and can be viewed round the clock.

The **Louis A. Turpen Aviation Museum**, in the International Terminal, is housed in a spacious, beautifully designed room rather than dispersed throughout SFO. Propeller-heads, take note: the aviation museum isn't all about planes. It's about the experience of traveling by air, encompassing the history and romance of flight. Built on the architectural footprint of SFO's 1937 terminal, the museum echoes that now-demolished terminal with a vaguely Moorish look, high ceilings, a mezzanine, and tiled floors.

The **International Terminal**, which cost just over $1 billion and was built while the rest of the airport continued to operate around it, is worth a look, even if you're not on an international flight. Check out the wavy, wing-like roofline designed by lead architect Craig Hartman and the glass-curtain front of the building. Then step inside the vast departures hall and look up at the oval light reflectors suspended from the ceiling: looking very much like UFOs awaiting permission to land, they constitute an artwork by James Carpenter. The art theme continues throughout the International Terminal, for which site-specific, large-scale works of public art were commissioned. Rigo's *Thinking of Balmy Alley* in boarding area G is a ceramic-tile mosaic that evokes the street murals in the city's Mission district (see Secret Murals).

There are, of course, many shopkeepers who will be delighted to sell you a souvenir while you wait for your flight or someone else's. For high-quality, non-kitschy merchandise, I recommend the San Francisco Museum of Modern Art's **MuseumStore**, located in the International Terminal. With its white-walled interior, the MuseumStore displays jewelry, art books, CD-ROMs, apparel, and branded SFMOMA goods to fine effect. The alternating black-and-gray-striped vinyl flooring recalls the striated marble floor of SFMOMA's downtown building. The store ships anywhere, and sells mostly small items that can fit into carry-on bags. If you're famished, **Harbor Village** has great dim sum and other Chinese food, and is also in the International Terminal.

SFO is located 15 miles south of San Francisco on the western shore of San Francisco Bay. At this writing, there is considerable construction there, since a BART rail line connecting the airport with downtown S.F. is being built and the old International Terminal is being converted to handle domestic flights. Congestion happens, both on the freeway and in the looming, crowded parking garages. If you're not running late, head to the rooftops to find a parking space.

A variety of commercial passenger vans carry people to and from SFO. The largest and most reliable company is **Supershuttle** (558-8500), which runs dark blue vans with gold lettering. You catch them outside the terminals on the top level. When going to the airport, call Supershuttle and reserve. For people leaving SFO, there are no reservations; you join the line. If you're taking a cab, you queue on the second level under the concrete roadway at a designated taxi stand. Fares to downtown should run about $30 (including tip).

SECRET
SKATING

Whether you're skating on wheels or blades, concrete or ice, there are plenty of places to skate in S.F., and businesses that will rent or sell you the equipment you need.

Inline skaters, roller skaters, skateboarders, and many others flock to **John F. Kennedy Drive** on Sundays and holidays, when this main traffic artery in the eastern end of Golden Gate Park is closed to motor vehicles. The result: a weekly people's festival on wheels. It's nice to take back a big piece of macadam in the grassy, tree-lined park and enjoy the day there. Runners, power walkers, moms pushing baby carriages — just about every type of person shares the street on Sundays. You can rent skateboards, roller skates, and inline skates (and snowboards, if you're heading up to the Sierra Nevada mountains) at **Skates on Haight** (1818 Haight St., 752-8375), near the eastern end of the park. Some skates can be modified for people with disabilities. Or head over to **Golden Gate Park Skate and Bike** (3038 Fulton St., 668-1117), which also has a large selection. Helmets and pads are included in the rental prices.

Inline skates have turned roller hockey into a popular big-city game, especially in snow-less cities like San Francisco, where ice hockey has a devoted but smallish following. **Bladium In-Line Hockey Rink** (1050 Third St., 442-5060) is a large, modern facility with leagues for players of all ages and both genders, plus a snack shop, changing rooms, showers, a cage where you can practice your amazing slap shot, and a place to rent equipment.

If they're not in Golden Gate Park, inline skaters and roller skaters who want to cover ground out of doors head to the **Embarcadero**, the promenade flanking the roadway of the same name between Bay and Townsend streets. Skateboarders also favor the Embarcadero for its ramps and broad surfaces, often congregating at **Justin Herman Plaza** at the foot of Market Street or on **Pier 7**. Pier 7, at the foot of Broadway, juts well out into the bay, providing great views of the water and the skyline. Skateboarders bust some moves here — and also, unfortunately, tear up some of the surfaces that the city spends a lot of money building and continually repairing.

Ice skaters can have a good time at **Yerba Buena Ice Skating Center** (750 Folsom St., 777-3727). The magnificent enclosed rooftop ice rink has humongous windows, so that even though you're indoors, the light and the views give you the feeling you're zipping along on an outdoor rink. You can rent skates there.

SECRET
SPECIALTY MUSEUMS

Should the major museums not supply enough art or history to suit your tastes — or should they not concentrate on your interests — the city's more specialized museums may be just the thing. So-called niche museums concentrate their attention on one subject, exploring it in depth.

San Francisco is well stocked with history museums. The **California Historical Society** (678 Mission St., 357-1848) runs a superb small museum in a renovated brick building. It mounts exhibitions on state history, from the Native American cultures that predated California proper, through the Mexican era, the arrival of the Americans, the Gold Rush, and the hyper-development of the Golden State, up to the present. Photographs, lithographs, books, oil paintings and watercolors, clothing, commercial and household objects — all are fodder for the museum, which additionally has a fine gift shop and bookstore with a good selection of children's books.

More Gold Rush memorabilia — including $20 gold coins, a stage-coach, and scrip issued as money by the 19th-century eccentric Emperor Norton — is on display, free, at the **Wells Fargo History Museum** (420 Montgomery St., 396-2619). The **Museum of the City**

of San Francisco (928-0289) is a peripatetic institution, installing exhibits in **City Hall** (200 Polk St.) and occasionally elsewhere. Its holdings of historical newspapers, photographs, and, inexplicably, movie projectors are extensive. The **Chinese Historical Society of America Museum** (644 Broadway, 391-1188) compiles Chinese American family trees and extensive background on Chinese immigration from the 1850s to the present, along with lectures and changing exhibits. The **San Francisco Performing Arts Library and Museum** (401 Van Ness Ave., fourth floor, 255-4800) has a thoroughly entertaining collection of theater memorabilia — playbills, posters, publicity photos, and the like — as well as costumes, scene designs, books, videos, and musical scores. The library is open by appointment. The **Jewish Museum of San Francisco** (591-8800) plans to move to the old Jessie Street Substation in 2003. That historical structure is being renovated to house the museum, which collects artifacts and contemporary art rooted in the Jewish experience.

The city stashes a treasure trove of specialty museums at **Fort Mason Center** (Laguna and Marina), on the northern waterfront. This former point of embarkation for U.S. troops in the Pacific theaters of World War II, the Korean War, and the Vietnam War, is now a thriving base for the arts community. No fewer than five non-profit museums are based at Fort Mason, which sprawls across five rehabbed former military buildings and into two old finger piers. I was editor of a now-defunct monthly arts magazine there in the '80s, and it was a pleasure to go to work at Fort Mason; it's in a beautiful locale and there's always something going on.

The **Museum of Craft and Folk Art** (Fort Mason Center, Building A, 775-0991) shows changing exhibitions that can cover anything from metalworking or cloth craftworks to Chinese children's hats. It's a delight. The **African-American Historical and Cultural**

Society Museum (Fort Mason Center, Building C, 441-0640) displays changing exhibitions on the black experience in America, with an emphasis on the pleasures and vicissitudes of everyday life. The **Mexican Museum** (Fort Mason Center, Building D, 202-9700) specializes in pre-Hispanic art, Chicano fine art, and Mexican colonial arts, among others, and has a fine gift shop with handcrafted jewelry. The Mexican Museum will relocate to new quarters near Yerba Buena Center in late 2003. The **Museo Italo-Americano** (Fort Mason Center, Building C, 673-2200) maintains a small gallery for visual arts by Italian and Italian American artists, has a nice gift shop, and offers Italian language lessons. The museum's permanent collection includes paintings and sculptures. A fifth museum, the **Maritime Museum**, maintains administrative headquarters at Fort Mason but berths its exhibitions in a waterside 1930s Art Deco building at the **Hyde Street Pier** (556-3002), where it forms part of the **San Francisco Maritime National Historical Park**, along with vintage ships at anchor. Even landlubbers can have fun learning about San Francisco's historical links to the sea.

For a more unusual museum experience, check out the **Levi Strauss Factory** (250 Valencia St., 565-9159). There are free tours of this working factory and company museum twice a week. It's all housed in a bright yellow 1906 wooden building on pretty, landscaped grounds adorned with flowers and palms.

Far from the flowers, on a smelly downtown block, you will find the engaging **Cartoon Art Museum** (814 Mission St., CAR-TOON). It occupies the second floor of the building, above a liquor store and several other businesses. The museum has 6,000 square feet of exhibition space, a kids' room, bookstore, and research library, along with impressive collections of original art. You can view animated cartoons on TV monitors as well as pencil and line drawings by the likes of Garry Trudeau, Matt Groening, Charles Schulz of *Peanuts* fame, and the great Walt Kelley, creator of *Pogo*, on the wall and in display cases.

SECRET

SPOKEN WORD

Spoken-word performances are like fireflies: they illuminate quickly and disappear. With this in mind, here are places to look for spoken-word events, poetry slams, or just plain old poetry readings, before they get here and go.

Surely the most beautiful place to hear readings and talks is the **Mechanics' Institute Library** (57 Post St., 393-0100), founded in 1854 and the city's oldest library. Housed in a landmark downtown building with huge windows that give clear views of the stacks from the street, the Mechanics Institute sponsors ambitious authors' programs, free to dues-paying members and open to the public at low cost. Writers like S.F. poet Janice Mirikitani, old China hand Orville Schell, and stylish popular culture writer Barnaby Conrad III have read at this inspiring place.

For attitude and edge, try the **Justice League** (628 Divisadero St., 289-2038), a nightclub that is home to both bands and DJs for late-night sessions. The Justice League hosts open-mike poetry sessions on the second Sunday of most months, and has hosted National Youth Poetry Slam events. It usually has DJs spinning and scratching behind the spoken-word performers.

More open-mike action can be had at **Hospitality House Community Arts Studio** (146 Leavenworth St., 749-2132), a non-profit outlet for street poets and others, some of whom are homeless. **Artspeak at Mission Badlands** (2811 Mission St., no listed phone) hosts a spoken-word series for new voices and has a nominal door charge. **Project Artaud** (450 Florida St., 621-7797), one of the city's major alternative-art performance venues, especially for dance, is also a vehicle for spoken-word work. **Brain Wash** (1122 Folsom St., 861-3663), a hip cafe and coin laundry South of Market, posts upcoming performance events on its bulletin board, as do community-minded bars and cafes. The weekly giveaway newspapers and the *Chronicle's* Datebook section, especially the Sunday Datebook, are good sources for calendars and related information.

S E C R E T
STREET FAIRS

Street fairs are a colorful, fun way to see the city and meet the locals. Most neighborhoods host street fairs, usually in summer or early fall, when the weather is good. All the fairs are free; most are crowded and interesting. Vendors will sell you crafts or food, but if you just want to stroll and look, that's fine, too.

Definitely the oldest street fair in San Francisco, and possibly in the United States, according to festival organizers, is the **North Beach Festival**. Founded in 1954 and held annually in June, the North Beach fest is a good-natured event that puts the city's most European neighborhood on display, with its sidewalk cafes, coffee roasters, wine bars, and restaurants. You can have an acid flashback, literally if you want, at the **Haight Street Fair**, where today's tattooed and nose-ringed locals mingle with the tie-dyed, gray-haired ponytails of the previous counterculture and artisans put their wares on offer. The most adult and outrageous fair is the **Folsom Street Fair** (861-3247 or www.folsomstreetfair.com), where leather-clad musclemen reign and gay culture is enshrined. This is the time and place to pick up that leather dog collar, and the person to wear it. The Folsom Street fest is not to be confused with those other big gay 'n' lesbian holidays: **Halloween**, with its costumed partying in the Civic Center, and the **Pride Parade**, held every June (see Secret Gay) in the Castro district and along Market Street. Additionally, there is the **Castro Street Fair** (467-3354), held in October.

The city celebrates its Hispanic heritage at **Carnaval**, a festive name borrowed from Rio's great party. This splashy Mission district event features a parade for happy exhibitionists with few inhibitions and few articles of clothing, along with hot music and spicy food. The Mexican **Cinco de Mayo** celebrates Mexico's victory over an invading French army in 1810, and is held in early May, not always right on May 5. **Fiesta Filipina** (650-757-4803) is staged in Civic Center Plaza annually in June to mark Philippines Independence Day. It is believed to be the largest Filipino American holiday party in the country.

San Francisco also puts on a major **Chinese New Year** parade and celebration, complete with traditional lion dances and a new Miss Chinatown, in late January or early February at the start of the lunar new year. In the fall, the **Autumn Moon Festival** spills out from the shops and restaurants along Grant Avenue in Chinatown. Because it's not as ballyhooed as Chinese New Year, this festival can be a less-crowded alternative to the bigger event. And it usually gets better weather, as it's not held in mid-winter.

SECRET
STREET PEOPLE

Maybe it's the guy who disguises himself as a bush and jumps out at you, expecting to be paid. Or maybe it's the dapper fellow who sits on the same spot every day and rails against pre-marital fornication with that fire and brimstone tone of conviction. Or maybe it's just that I've been spare-changed while jogging by a panhandler who ran with me for half a block delivering his spiel. (And he didn't get winded, which is more than I can say for myself.) I don't know what it is, but San Francisco seems to have more street people — whether they're literally "homeless" or not — per square inch than anyplace on Earth, and I've been to Jakarta, Borneo, rural China, and other places where people are far poorer than they are in the United States.

Inquiring minds want to know, and reasonable people may differ, about why the streets of San Francisco appear to be so crowded with people conducting animated conversations with invisible companions. It's the temperate climate, some say (although human beings have frozen to death trying to sleep on the street). It's S.F.'s liberal tolerance (or guilt) that shames people into giving money, thus encouraging more begging. It's generous social welfare benefits. It's our mystical emanations beckoning people to come hither and plop down. Whatever the reason, they're out there. Here is a short guide to the most interesting folks on the street.

The **look-I'm-a-bush guy** works the sidewalk along Jefferson Street at Fisherman's Wharf, in wait for unsuspecting tourists. He hides behind a bouquet of branches and leaves, spots a prospect, then vigorously shakes his limbs at them and emits a sharp cry. He expects to be paid for this singular skill but doesn't usually object if he's not. The

anti-fornication guy sits on a stool near the cable car turnaround at Powell and Market streets with a placard. He repeats a memorized spiel to the effect that sex is supposed to be between a virgin woman and a virgin man, and if it isn't that makes "the woman a whore and the man a whore-monger." At 5 p.m. or so, the well-dressed man politely takes his leave, then returns the next day to the same spot. He clearly sees this as his job, although he doesn't ask for money.

There's an **impeach Clinton guy** all around town who is not your run-of-the-mill critic of Bill's politics or libido. No, this fellow — also nicely dressed and carrying a sign that reads "Impeach Clinton. 12 Galaxies. Guiltied to a Technitronic Rocket Society" — has motivations of a more cosmic nature. Therefore, I have cited him twice in this book; he also appears in the Not of This Earth category. He doesn't ask for money but spends much of his time on city streets.

Well, you get the idea. Of course, most street people don't have clearly worked-out personas like these three. They hang out in encampments in Civic Center Plaza, along Mission Street near Seventh Street (north side), under bridges, and in public parks, including Hallidie Plaza near the Visitors Center. Most are not dangerous but can be unpleasantly persistent. Be kind, and watch your back.

SECRET
SUNDAY BRUNCH

Practically every restaurant in town with a sentient being in management or marketing serves a Sunday brunch, but there are Sunday brunches and there are Sunday brunches.

If you want to go vertical, you have several good, if pricey, brunches on the lazy-Sunday menu. The aptly named Cityscape restaurant at the **San Francisco Hilton Hotel** (333 O'Farrell St., 923-5002) feeds you extravagantly in its **Tower One** 46th-floor aerie. Pray for a clear day. If you're above or in the clouds, clouds are all you'll see. Otherwise, there's a sweeping view from bay to shining sea. Food? There's an all-you-can-eat buffet for $44 per head. Featured are morsels like Hawaiian chicken salad with papaya, macadamia nuts, and ginger, and traditional brunch fare like eggs benedict. Another choice vertical brunch is served in the **Carnelian Room** at the **Bank of America Center** (555 California St., 433-7500). How high is it? We're talking 52 stories. Again, there are sweeping, 360-degree, water-to-water views (provided nature cooperates) and lavish food, including Dungeness crab cakes, foie gras, Grand Marnier soufflé — that kind of thing. Price: $30 per person. Verticality also lives in the **Crown Room** of the **Fairmont Hotel** (950 Mason St., 772-5000), high atop Nob Hill. Indulgence lives, too, with eggs benedict, oysters, mussels, omelets, cheesecake, and more. Price: $38.50.

For more down-to-earth prices at a down-to-earth location, you can't do better than **Ella's** (500 Presidio Ave., 441-5669). Prices will be less than half of those for the high-rise brunches (of course, without the views). Ella's is welcoming and pleasant: big but not cavernous, with lots of natural light, and lots of bustle in the restaurant's two rooms. Be prepared to wait. Take the Sunday paper along to read and share. Try the buttermilk pancakes or the chicken hash with eggs. Or the fried cornmeal with cheddar and scallions served with eggs. Or the brandied-orange French toast. This is a great breakfast place seven days a week.

There are other very good places, to be sure. **Mama's** (1701 Stockton St., 362-6421) serves American comfort food in a pleasant corner location on Washington Square. Despite the cutesy name, the food is good, especially the omelets and home fries. **Doidge's** (2217 Union St., 921-2149) is an upscale eatery on the upscale shopping strip of Union Street; it's been popular with locals for a long time and is always crowded. For continental flair, try **Absinthe Restaurant & Bar** (398 Hayes St., 551-1590). Absinthe is lovely, lined with vintage French posters and photos, fronted by big windows, and graced with zinc-topped tables, cane chairs, pressed-tin ceilings. Absinthe serves elegant wines and liquors (though not the lethal drink it's named for). The light, fluffy omelet with smoked salmon, cherry tomatoes, herbs, and crème fraîche is highly recommended. So is the French toast with ricotta filling and apricot compote. And — very important — the coffee is fresh and strong. For that end-of-the-continent feeling, go to the **Cliff House** (1090 Point Lobos Ave., 386-3330). The lure of the Cliff House is the view of ocean and sky more than the food, but the hot popovers are good. Leave your name and be ready to wait; they'll call you for one of a number of possible rooms in this big, shambling building. **Valentine's Cafe** (1793 Church St., 285-2257), in Noe Valley, serves a brunch with a twist: it's vegan, for the meat free and milk free.

S E C R E T

SURFING

You've got your woodie, your board, your Beach Boys and Jan and Dean tapes, even your Dick Dale (king of surf guitar) CD, and you're looking for the great surfing beaches. Look for them 400 miles south of here, in L.A. Or five hours by jet plane west of here, on the north shore of Oahu, Hawaii. Those are great surfing beaches, and they have warm water.

San Francisco can't match those surfing heavens, but people do surf in S.F. They just have to wear wetsuits to handle the water, which, at 50 degrees or so, is cold indeed. Most surfers go to **Ocean Beach**, the three-mile-long strand along the Pacific. Ocean Beach gets waves that come out of nowhere and crest at 20 feet high, so it's no place for a novice and no place to fool around. It's best to have experience before getting into the water here, and to surf with friends. **Fort Point**, just inside the Golden Gate Bridge on the San Francisco side, is another favorite spot for local surfers. A popular place to buy gear, including long and short surfboards, is **Wise Surfboards** (800 Great Hwy., 750-9473). Owner Bob Wise opened the shop in 1968 and sells boards for anywhere from $350 to $1,000.

S E C R E T
SWANK
❀

The IPO went great. You figured out how to deliver eternal life over the Internet, and now you're filthy rich. You've got it. You're gonna flaunt it. You're thinking swank.

The **Ritz-Carlton Hotel** (600 Stockton St., 296-7465) will let its opulent **Presidential Suite** go for $3,800. It is 1960 square feet of luxury with a 1200-square-foot balcony. Failing that, you could book a package at the Ritz-Carlton. They have one that includes round-trip transportation from SFO or Oakland airport, a chauffeured limousine tour of romantic S.F. spots (including the Palace of Fine Arts and secluded Baker Beach), a bottle of chilled champagne (you keep the toasting flutes), and overnight accommodations in a Club Deluxe room. Club Deluxe includes the services of a dedicated concierge, express checkout, high-speed Internet access, and a special elevator to your floor. Cost? Need you ask?

The **Penthouse Suite** at the **Fairmont Hotel** (California and Mason, 772-5000) is a steal at $8,000 a night. For that you get a billiard room designed in Persian motifs with inlaid mosaics, the serene circular library where Ronald Reagan met Mikhail Gorbachev, a luxurious, salmon-hued dining room, and the terrace where Sean Connery appeared in *The Rock*. And you'll have the satisfaction of knowing that your fellow penthouse guests have included John F. Kennedy and Prince Charles. Or, you could have afternoon tea in the beautifully restored Laurel Court restaurant, with champagne and caviar, for $45 per person, thus saving $7,900 or so.

The **Hotel Palomar** (12 Fourth St., 348-1111) can help with romance, as well as business — all in swanky style, of course. The Palomar has a Pop the Question package at $675 per night. It includes overnight accommodations in a king suite, a step-by-step marriage proposal booklet, a cocktail in the bar for courage, a chilled bottle of champagne (natch), a limo pick-up for the prospective bride, and breakfast for two the next morning. Of course, dinner in the Palomar's fine-dining restaurant, the **Fifth Floor** (348-1555), might work just as well. The food is French and very fine, and the decor is très sophisticated and assured, with foie gras, caviar, lobster, and the usual caloric suspects on the menu. The restaurant opened in late 1999, and executive chef George Morrone's interpretation of modern French has made it madly popular.

Romantic atmosphere is definitely on the menu at **Fleur de Lys** (777 Sutter St., 673-7779), a high-end French destination restaurant run

by its chef and owner, Herbert Keller. I dined here once in a group
that included a senior executive from the Hotel Ritz in London, who
adored the food and characterized the service as "quiet and correct."
That was high praise, indeed. This is a favorite for couples in thrall to
Cupid.

Masa's (648 Bush St., 989-7154) has been one of the city's premier
restaurants for two decades, and it is far from tired. The food here,
too, is French, and beautifully prepared. Dinner for two, with wine,
will run about $100 per person, and will be unforgettably good.
Aqua (252 California St., 956-9662) is an elegant seafood restaurant
with an exceptionally fine wine list, huge picture windows facing the
street, high ceilings, big vases of fresh flowers, and a happening bar.
Aqua has no street sign to speak of, so look closely for the address.
For a dream of Asian big-city decadence with a smoky jazz beat,
there is **Shanghai 1930** (133 Steuart St., 896-5600). You enter by
descending a hushed flight of stairs, glide into the stylish main dining
room with its sleek bar, and dine on refined cuisine — Chinese, but
with subtle Western accents.

If you want just a drink, there is no way to top the **Garden Court**
of the **Sheraton Palace Hotel** (2 New Montgomery St., 512-1111)
for swank. Once the driveway for horse-drawn carriages, the courtyard was enclosed and topped by a beautiful glass dome after the
earthquake and fire of 1906. In the 1990s, the Garden Court and the
rest of the hotel underwent a sparkling renovation. The dome gleams
with natural light now, the potted palms give the room a Gay Nine-
ties touch (that's the 1890s), and you'll definitely feel you've arrived.
If you want to arrive from on high, book a room at the high-rise
Mandarin Oriental Hotel (222 Sansome St., 276-9888) and sip
champagne in bathtubs above the clouds before windows that go all
the way to the floor. No one can see you — you're too high up —

but you can see the whole city. You have the option of bathing in champagne or taking a milk bath. The pinnacle of luxury in this hotel is the Oriental Suite on the 38th floor, available for $3,000 per night.

SECRET

TAIWANESE
PEARL DRINKS

If this sweet, surprisingly complex, refreshing drink hasn't hit your town yet, you can try it here first. It's an acquired taste that I have managed to acquire while scouring the city for the best version. I haven't found a flat-out winner yet, but Asian restaurants and shops all over town make their own versions of this drink, which first became popular in Taiwan.

The pearls in a pearl milk tea are tapioca balls, small or large, white or black. The tea is black tea. The milk is either regular milk from the carton or condensed milk. Ice is added. Everything is whipped into a froth. Then you get a cup with a lid on top, and a fat, fluorescent plastic straw for sucking up all that sweet tapioca from the bottom.

One good place for pearl milk tea is **Assia Cafe** (336 Kearny St., 398-2388), a hole-in-the-wall Vietnamese restaurant that makes its own versions of the drink. You can get it with Thai tea (chai), which is not quite as strong as black tea. The watermelon tapioca drink is refreshing, and the white tapioca mango coconut drink is really good, too. The white tapioca pearls are smaller, easier to swallow, and more familiar to Westerners than black tapioca, which is large but soft and chewy and still pretty easy to swallow. The wonderfully named **Wonderful Foods Company** (2110 Irving St., 731-6889) makes a killer pearl milk tapioca tea with added lychee-nut flavor, mixed behind the counter rather like a milkshake. This snack shop also sells Asian candies, such as sweetened ginger. The **Taiwan Restaurant** (289 Columbus Ave., 989-6789 or 445 Clement St., 387-1789) makes a good milk tea with the grapeshot-sized black tapioca pearls. The restaurants are well located, in North Beach near old Chinatown and in the new Chinatown in the Richmond district, should you want to explore those vibrant areas with a refreshing drink in your hand. **Mandalay** (4344 California St., 386-3895), a low-priced, high-quality Burmese restaurant, makes a very good tapioca drink by combining large white tapioca pearls with shredded coconut. In yet another variation, **Alpenglo Tea** (401 Sansome St., 986-4206) will add pearls to black tea, Earl Grey, green tea, and more. Warning: this yummy Taiwanese import can become addictive.

SECRET
TAQUERIAS

You want the basics in a taqueria: good, cheap food that surprises you once in a while with a twist on standard-issue Mexican. If the taqueria is fast and goes lightly on the grease, that's good, too.

With its sizable Mexican American community and historic ties to Mexico — California and S.F. were part of Mexico before the U.S. wrested away the Southwest in the Mexican–American War — San Francisco has no shortage of taquerias. But, of course, you only want to know about the good ones.

The best place in town from the standpoint of freshness and clean, piquant tastes is **El Toro** (598 Valencia St., 431-3351). It costs a little more than other Mission district taquerias, but it's a bright, cheery place in a corner location, with the best salsa and really flavorful fast food. The burrito supremo is a meal in itself that will hold most people all day. El Toro has Mexican and American beer, and Mexican fruit drinks longer on sugar water than fruit juice. A mariachi band wanders in from time to time to play Spanish tunes, upbeat yet tinged with melancholy.

The best value for money is **La Cumbre** (515 Valencia St., 863-8205), which has food nearly as good as El Toro's. Prices are low enough to make you weep, and the chicken, beef, and pork — grilled as you line up cafeteria-style to place your order — is of high quality. La Cumbre is bigger than most Mission district taquerias, so you can usually get a seat. Check out the wall poster with the bosomy senorita smiling broadly while hoisting the Mexican flag and making revolution. Not all the salsa is in the food at La Cumbre.

Another good value for money place is **Gordo** (three S.F. locations). The chicken is all white meat and virtually greaseless, and the salsa is fresh and mouthwatering with a nice balance between hot chilis and cooling cilantro. If you want to eat sitting down, go to **Gordo no. 6** at 5450 Geary Boulevard (668-8226); the others are cramped, basic take-out places. **El Balazo** (two locations) sells full meals at 1980s prices, with sides of cabbage salad, guacamole, sour cream, and salsa. The chicken mole is especially good, and there are a lot of vegetarian items. Look hard: El Balazo's downtown location (54 Mint St., 882-9575) is tucked away behind the old U.S. Mint at Fifth and Mission streets and is easy to miss. **El Farolito** (2777 Mission St., 826-4870) is a long, dark, narrow lunch counter popular with local Latinos but not especially well frequented by non-Hispanics. It serves good carne asada (steak), as well as beef variations (head meat, tongue, and brains being among them).

SECRET
TATTOOS

You're ready for the millennium. You're pierced. You're shaved. Almost everything's perfect, save for one thing: no ink on your skin. Sadly, inexplicably, you lack tattoos. Fear not. This can be rectified. **Lyle Tuttle Tattooing** (841 Columbus Ave., 775-4991) will be happy to adorn your skin with dragons, clouds, a heart with an arrow through it, or nearly anything else its namesake and owner Lyle Tuttle, a longtime S.F. tattoo artist, can dream up. The same goes for the reassuringly named **Mom's Body Shop** (1408 Haight St., 864-6667), which offers Japanese-style tattoos and American body art. Here, as in most tattoo studios, each resident artist has a portfolio that you can scan before choosing the design you want and the artist to create it. Just a block or two away, another Haight-Ashbury place, **Anubis Warpus** (1525 Haight St., 431-2218), will adorn you with edgy designs, as well as provide piercing on demand. San Francisco is a tattoo town; the S.F. Yellow Pages lists 25 city businesses offering tattooing, some no more than scuzzy storefronts. Wherever you go, the dangers of non-sterilized needles need hardly be emphasized; make sure the place has been certified by the S.F. Department of Health and can prove it. If you're interested in the history of body art, check out the small **Tattoo Museum** in the front of Lyle Tuttle's North Beach shop. Tuttle has collected designs from the early 20th century, and even the 19th, and the scope is international.

SECRET
TEA

I once interviewed James Norwood Pratt, the author of *The Tea Lover's Treasury*, at the Imperial Tea Court. While sipping an elegant black tea brewed from loose leaves in a porcelain cup, he commented, "In our time, in America, where we are so bereft of any means with which to feed our spirit, I believe the thirst for tea is nothing less than a craving for beauty in our lives. Society is constantly telling you, 'Hurry up, hurry up.' Tea says 'Slow down.'"

The **Imperial Tea Court** (1411 Powell St., 788-6080 or 800-567-5898) is the perfect place for philosophical musing. Indeed, it is the most beautiful and interesting spot in the city for savoring tea and, as Pratt said, unplugging and slowing down. Run by a couple from Beijing who say it was the first traditional Chinese tea room in America, the Imperial Tea Court has marble floors, rosewood paneled walls, and singing birds in wooden cages placed around the premises. Outside is the tumult of Chinatown and the roar of traffic; inside are elegant tables and chairs and displays of bulk teas on offer: eshan pekoe, jade fire, gunpowder, and dragon whiskers among the unfermented green teas; orchid oolong and imperial wu yi yan cha among the semi-fermented oolongs; Yunnan supreme, Shanghai Nights blend, and red mu dan among the fermented black teas. Rare barely fermented white tea, scented tea (like the exquisite jasmine blossom, which consists of tight pearls of jasmine flowers brewed in the teapot at your table), and herbal teas are also available.

There are other places in Chinatown to sip or buy tea, of course. While none can match the Imperial Tea Court, some are interesting in their own right. Among these is **Ten Ren Tea Company** (949 Grant Ave., 362-0656), where you sit on carved stools and teas are kept in gold canisters.

Several grand venues offer afternoon tea and high tea in the English manner. The lobby lounge at the **Ritz-Carlton Hotel** (600 Stockton St., 296-7465) pours a proper British tea made from loose leaves, which brings out the flavor better than teabags. The **Rotunda** at **Neiman Marcus** (150 Stockton St., 362-4777), an elegant restaurant beneath a historic stained glass dome, has a nice selection of regular and herbal teas, served with sweets, tiny scones, jam, and butter; try to sit along the curved windows overlooking Union Square with its graceful palm trees and buzzing shopaholics. A much less grand and less expensive alternative is the **King George Hotel** (334 Mason St., 781-5050). The hotel's **Windsor Tea Room** is a small mezzanine space where you can get little crust-less sandwiches, clotted cream, and the works, though it doesn't have a massive amount of charm.

The most unusual place for European teas — and it's virtually unknown, even to locals — is **Tal-y-Tara Tea and Polo Shoppe** (6439 California St., 751-9275). When the Meakins, the shop's proprietors, were wondering what to do with their teashop and their store for horse fanciers a few years back, they decided to combine both family businesses in a single location. The result is Tal-y-Tara, where you sip teas and nibble finger sandwiches amidst displays of bridles, saddles, riding boots, and horse-country magazines, and the not-unpleasant aroma of leather goods. Keep your eye peeled for this place; it's secreted on a residential block in the outer Richmond district. **Lovejoy's English Tea Room** (1351 Church St., 648-5895) is another offbeat place. Lovejoy's serves high tea all day in a space filled with antique furniture for sale.

Of course, it's tough to get anyone to slow down, let alone sit down, in speed- and convenience-crazed America, where sugary ice tea and big-gulp canned teas resembling soft drinks rule. Accordingly, there are many tea-to-go places around town. **A Cuppa Tea** (50 Post St., 986-9958) has a wide range of caffeinated teas, decaf varieties of favorites, such as English breakfast and Earl Grey, herbal teas, and supposedly health-giving green teas. Look for A Cuppa Tea on the second level of the Crocker Galleria mall. And look for its very American version of scones on the counter; they're as big as Frisbees. Another popular place for take-out tea is **Alpenglo Tea Company** (401 Sansome St., 986-4206), with its bright corner location in the financial district. Alpenglo has a few teas in stock that were supposedly grown organically, as well as tapioca pearls for sweetening your tea. Their green tea latte is rich, smooth, and incredibly good. Try it with ice on a hot San Francisco September afternoon.

The best of the to-go places is **Peet's Coffee & Tea** (nine S.F. locations, 800-999-2132). Peet's began with a single Berkeley store in 1966, founded by Alfred Peet, who apprenticed in his father's coffee and tea business in Holland and worked as a professional tea taster in Java. Although Peet's stores sell a lot of coffee, they are excellent sources for fine teas, too, perhaps reflecting the interests of Alfred Peet, who told me in an interview, "If you hung me upside down to find out what I know about coffee and tea, more [knowledge about] tea would fall out." Green, oolong, and black teas are sold at Peet's by the ounce, and you can buy hot or cold tea by the cup, of course.

Should you be looking for bulk tea to take home, try the **Whole Foods** alternative-foods supermarket (1765 California St., 674-0500), which sells some teas said to be organically grown, as well as herbal blends and regular teas.

SECRET
TEQUILAS

There must be dozens of places that have your basic tequila-drinking drill down cold: the salt on the back of the hand, the Jose Cuervo Gold down the hatch, the lime to suck on. All well and good, but the selection of tequilas — not to mention the quality of the drink — varies only slightly from place to place, with just a few exceptions.

One notable one is **Cafe Marimba** (2317 Chestnut St., 776-1506). Cafe Marimba doesn't look that promising from the street. It's located on a highly yuppified block of Chestnut in yuppie central, the Marina district, setting up expectations of college guys getting bodacious to impress their dates, and everyone trying out their fractured Spanish to show they were once in Oaxaca. But Cafe Marimba confounds these expectations. The Mexican regional food is good — tasty morsels that aren't swimming in lard, nice moles, swordfish tacos with mango salsa. The real surprises, though, are the tequilas, several dozen of them. Most are very fine; some are good enough to sip and compare as you would with any fine whiskey or wine. The place is loud, the service friendly. The tequilas make it worthwhile.

The true shrine of San Francisco tequilas, however, is a decidedly no-frills Mexican eatery in the outer Richmond district: **Tommy's Mexican Restaurant** (5929 Geary Blvd., 387-4747). Tommy's stocks top-of-the-line blue agave tequilas, personally selected by the owner, Tomas Bermejo, who hails from the Yucatan and revisits Mexico for the express purpose of finding new tequilas. He is said to have the largest selection outside Mexico. If you're drinking margaritas, the lime juice will be hand squeezed by the bartenders. Tequila tasting goes on nightly at the bar, where there are maybe eight stools. The food service is friendly, fast, and efficient, and the food is hearty and reasonably priced. But it's tequilas, close to 150 blue agave varieties, that make Tommy's special. In the small, somewhat dark restaurant, folks chow down and talk about the comparative merits of the engines of various Camaros. At the bar, purists in nice sweaters sip rare tequilas. For the scholarly, Tommy's offers a Tequila Master degree, with a T-shirt and framed certificate. You sample a wide range of tequilas and furrow your brow a lot to get it. And Tommy's would rather that you not drink the blended mainstream stuff there. Order Cuervo Gold and they charge you extra, for real.

SECRET
THEATER

San Francisco is a lively and sometimes arresting center for American regional theater, with a decided preference for off-center work. The city's most established company, **American Conservatory Theater** (415 Geary St., 749-2228), presents new plays and revivals in a renovated theater and graduates young thespians from its acting school. Danny Glover and Annette Bening are alumni of ACT, which has been revived artistically in recent years, and has presented U.S. premieres by Tom Stoppard, Britain's leading playwright of ideas, a year or two after opening in London.

Even older than ACT, though much less mainstream, is the **San Francisco Mime Troupe** (285-1717), a radical theater that creates a new play every summer and mounts performances outdoors in Bay Area parks. The actors pass the hat at the end of shows. Much loved and respected for its multicultural, leftish politics and artistic cheek, the Mime Troupe was founded in the 1960s by Ronnie Davis, draws strength from longtime chief playwright Joan Holden, and tours the world. Actor Peter Coyote is an alum. In recent years, the Mime Troupe has been at times uninspired. But a rousing Mime Troupe show is a very San Francisco experience and raises the spirit when the group is at the top of its game.

The **Magic Theatre** (Fort Mason Center, Building D, 441-8822) is another 1960s institution that continues to premiere new plays. The Magic had a long and productive run with Sam Shepard as playwright-in-residence in the late 1970s and early 1980s, when he wrote *True West*, *Tooth of Crime*, and other important plays. Another S.F. theater that blossomed in the 1980s, but has struggled since, relocating around town several times, is the **Eureka Theatre** (215 Jackson St., 788-SHOW). The Eureka premiered Tony Kushner's Pulitzer Prize-winning *Angels in America* and introduced British playwright Caryl Churchill to West Coast audiences. It has been less accomplished of late but still presents readings of new plays and fully mounted shows, some by visiting companies.

Many of the city's new works, solo shows, and alternative performances are presented in half a dozen small venues, usually with very reasonable ticket prices and usually located in the Mission district or the Tenderloin. The 70-seat **Intersection for the Arts** (446 Valencia St., 626-3311) has been around, at various sites, since 1965, and is always a good place to see interdisciplinary work, performance poetry, theater pieces, jazz, and such. The **Marsh** (1062 Valencia St., 826-5750) is a little bigger, with 110 seats, and is a center for new, socially conscious work; the gifted comic playwright and actor Charlie Varon often appears there. **Exit Theatre** (156 Eddy St., 673-3847) has three

tiny black-box spaces, an intimate feel, and new work on stage. The **New Conservatory Theatre** (25 Van Ness Ave., 861-8972) is a small, polished venue for new pieces, often gay and lesbian themed. Other places to check for new and edgy fare are **Venue 9** (252 Ninth St., 289-2000), which stages performance poetry, jazz, and readings; **Il Teatro 450** (449 Powell St., 433-1172), home of the Working Women Festival and some Fringe Festival shows; and **Thick House** (1695 18th St., 401-8081), the home of theater company Thick Description, which is rented out when Thick Description isn't doing its own shows.

The **San Francisco Fringe Festival** takes place in September, usually tapping Il Teatro 450 and Exit Theatre as prime performance venues. The Fringe Fest hasn't had the impact of the big fringe dos in Edinburgh and elsewhere, but it's worth taking a chance on, given that you might see something really new. You aren't likely to see anything groundbreaking at the **San Francisco Shakespeare Festival** (422-2222), but this celebration of the Bard is engaging enough. Shakespeare in the Park blooms in summer. The shows, produced by the S.F. Shakespeare Festival, are priced attractively: they're free.

Touring productions of Broadway hits are not uncommon. Some of the city's ornate old theaters are used for Carole Shorenstein Hays' Best of Broadway series and other touring shows. You can find same-day, half-price tickets to shows at the **Tix Bay Area** booth on the Stockton Street side of Union Square (433-7827). Otherwise, big-show tickets are available from **Ticketmaster** (421-2700 or 421-8497) for heritage theaters, such as the Orpheum, Curran, Marines Memorial, and Golden Gate Theatre, all located near downtown or in the Tenderloin.

TOURIST TRAPS

One man's ceiling is another man's floor. In keeping with this, one person's tourist trap is another person's good time. Broadly speaking, though, San Franciscans agree that certain places are mainly for tourists, not for themselves. Few locals have much to do with **Fisherman's Wharf**, which has only a precious few commercial fishing operations. Locals go there chiefly when our family and friends arrive from out of town and want to go. Our reasons for avoidance have to do with gawking crowds, lousy fast food, a plague of T-shirt and trinket shops hawking inexpensive but poorly made merchandise, and a general atmosphere of cheesiness.

Still, there are interesting places amidst the cheese. If you find yourself on the northern waterfront at Fisherman's Wharf, or nearby attractions, such as Ghirardelli Square and Pier 39, you can scope out some good stuff. Even in the tacky heart of the wharf, you can sometimes catch a decent blues band at **Lou's Pier 47** (300 Jefferson St., 771-5687).

At **Pier 39**, a wholly rebuilt wooden finger pier littered with undistinguished shops, check out the **Eagle Cafe** (433-3689). The Eagle is an old waterfront joint that was popular with longshoremen and railway workers back when S.F. had a working waterfront and before it become a de facto theme park in the late 1960s. The Eagle was picked up and moved intact to its present location on Pier 39's second level. It serves food but — this is important — Do Not Order The Food. Instead, grab an alcoholic or non-alcoholic beverage of your choice and nurse it while you drink in the water views. The very best time to go to the Eagle is on a blustery, rainy winter's day. Sit there

and dream while storms roll in from the Pacific, and soak up a connection to the city's maritime past.

Most "attractions" at Pier 39 are unattractive. The **Underwater World** aquarium, for example, is known among locals as Underwhelming World. The same goes for some of **Ghirardelli Square** (900 North Point St.), although the handsomely restored former factory where Ghirardelli chocolate used to be made is a great place for people watching. If ennui sets in, scan the informative historic markers near the redbrick buildings (it's a multi-level complex, not a true square). Or duck into **Builders Booksource** (440-5773), a big and good bookstore with picture books and instructional stuff ranging from architecture books to do-it-yourself manuals. If your sweet tooth won't be denied, give in at the **Ghirardelli Soda Fountain & Chocolate Shop** (474-1414). They make pricey but good sundaes; try a Fog Horn (two scoops of chocolate, hot fudge sauce, raspberry sauce, chocolate chips, and whipped cream).

Just south and west of Ghirardelli is **The Cannery**, a nicely renovated former Del Monte peach cannery. Despite the crowds, the redbrick Cannery is still a peachy place, popular with tourists but with retail and restaurants a cut or two above the neighborhood norm. If you are musical, or looking for a gift, pop into **Lark in the Morning** (2801 Leavenworth St., 922-4277), a lovely shop with musical instruments for sale, most of them acoustic, such as lutes and dulcimers.

Tourist traps tend to border the cable car lines, cluster in San Francisco International Airport (many high-quality shops in the new International Terminal notwithstanding), or crowd Broadway from Grant Avenue to the Embarcadero; a "garlic restaurant" in North Beach seems to exist as much to sell branded souvenir food items, caps, and T-shirts as anything else, thanks to the garlic gimmick. Some of the expense-account places near Moscone Center are tourist traps in their own way. Such places exist to lure conventioneers with upscale dining "concepts." Of course, sometimes a concept is just a gimmick with attitude.

S E C R E T

USED BOOKS

From the moment I saw the sleeping cat in the window at **Abandoned Planet** (518 Valencia St., 861-4695), I knew I was home. Slightly musty, with a zanily uneven floor under a skylight illuminating the interior, this Mission district way station for used books is one of the city's best places for bargains and discoveries. On a table stacked high with books, I saw a used copy of the first book I wrote (Shameless Plug Department: *A Trumpet to Arms: Alternative Media in America/ South End Press*), thus confirming the sound judgment of the bookstore, if not the original owner of the copy.

In an era in which chain stores and the Internet are taking a stiff toll on brick-and-mortar stores, San Francisco still has a healthy quotient of independent bookstores, including places that specialize in used and hard-to-find volumes. In future, they may dwindle to a precious few or even disappear, but for now the choices are many and varied.

Some used bookstores try to cover their bets by selling other things, too, which may be a wise move. **Bird & Beckett Books & Records** (2788 Diamond St., 586-3733) is, as its name indicates, a source for recordings as well as books, and is valued by jazz collectors and fans of vinyl. **Books and Bookshelves** (99 Sanchez St., 621-3761), as its name indicates, sells not only used books but pine shelves to put them on; it sells furniture, too, unfinished to keep prices down. **Dog Eared**

Books (900 Valencia St., 282-1901) is another mix 'n' match store, selling new and used books, in addition to music. The **Bookmonger** (2411 Clement St., 387-2332) is a bit more pure; this unassuming little shop sells only ink on paper: used books and vintage magazines. This is the place to go if you want an issue of *Life* magazine from the 1960s with a cover story on the Mercury 7 astronauts. In fact, the Bookmonger seems so lost in time that it uses a manual cash register.

For unsurpassed strangeness, you have to stop by **McDonald's Book Shop** (48 Turk St., 673-2235). Located on one of the weirdest, toughest blocks of the Tenderloin, McDonald's is a barn of a bookstore, claiming to have one million books inside. Who's to say it doesn't? You could never count them all, or indeed, uncover them all. The dusty stacks would require a truly Herculean effort to clean; the stables were easy compared to this. But in its way, this place is great.

Antiquarian books live on in an amazing hive of bookstores at **49 Geary St.**, near Market. This building, which also houses a number of art galleries, bunches five dealers in rare, out-of-print, previously owned books and manuscripts on the same floor. The stores are **John Windle Antiquarian Bookseller** (986-5826); **Robert Dagg Rare Books** (989-6811); **Brick Row Bookshop** (398-0414); **Thomas A. Goldwasser Rare Books** (981-4100); and **Jeffrey Thomas Fine & Rare Books** (956-3272).

Nearly lost amid the restaurants, cafes, and honky-tonks of North Beach is **Carroll's Books** (633 Vallejo St., 397-6364), which appears to be little known even to the locals. This should change. Carroll's is a good store, beginning with the decor — including a birdcage with four delicate, singing finches — and continuing to the most important thing, the books. I found a book on the Spanish conquest of Mexico, reconstructed from rare fragments of writings by Aztec intellectuals, and bought this unique and intriguing volume for a song.

I have deliberately saved the best for last. The monarch of San Francisco used bookstores is **Green Apple Books** (506 Clement St., 387-2272). Green Apple is actually two close-together storefronts in the inner Richmond district. From its friendly name to its knowledgeable and helpful staff and its large and diverse stock of books, recordings, and magazines, this store is a gem. It has wooden floors and rough-hewn wooden shelves, of course. You may browse as long as you like, of course. Feed your mind at Green Apple, then feed your body at the New Golden Turtle (see Secret Vietnamese) a block away. Incidentally, Green Apple has a branch in the inner Sunset, also a good source for used books, called **Ninth Avenue Books** (1348 Ninth Ave., 665-2938). In the same business district near Ninth and Irving is a branch of Berkeley's estimable **Black Oak Books** (630 Irving St., 564-0877), which seldom disappoints.

S E C R E T
VEGETARIAN

Greens: a form of vegetable, the leafy kind, and the name of the best vegetarian restaurant in the city, probably one of the best in any city. **Greens** (Fort Mason Center, Building A, 771-6222) has redefined vegetarian cuisine since it opened in 1979. Luxury, not austerity or sacrifice, is the watchword here, with rich desserts, absolutely fresh vegetables (many grown for the restaurant at its Green Gulch Farm), and one of the best wine lists anywhere showing the way. Situated right on the water, Greens has an unbeatable view of the bay and the Golden Gate Bridge. After sunset, the restaurant puts candles on the tables in its high-ceilinged dining room; from the outside, it looks warmly, softly inviting through the huge windows. Operated by the San Francisco Zen Center, Greens used to use Zen students as its wait staff. They were so spacey, you expected your server to find satori well before you got your pastry turnover with zucchini, corn, and asiago cheese. The wait staff is less Zenned-out now, so Greens' service almost matches the exquisite food.

Millennium (246 McAllister St., 487-9800) comes close to equaling Greens. The fact that Millennium is vegan and uses no animal by-products makes that feat all the more impressive. Located on two levels in the Abigail Hotel, Millennium offers wines said to be organic, very good grain-based dishes, and some of the soy and vegetable meatless "meat" dishes I've never understood or found appealing. If you want meat, eat meat. If you want vegetarian, eat vegetables, fruit, and grains. Still, the cooking here is accomplished.

Another high-end vegetarian destination restaurant is **Joubert's** (4115 Judah St., 753-5448). Run by natives of South Africa, Joubert's serves highly spiced lentil and vegetable dishes inspired by South African cooking. It also stocks a small but good selection of South African wines, many by the glass, or by the bottle for taking home. A long ramp leads from street level to a second-level room with a gas fire-place. The staff is knowledgeable and attentive without rushing you. Try the piesang garong (baked banana in curried peanut atjaar, served with curried rice, peanuts, and raisins).

Other prime veggie places include **Herbivore** (983 Valencia St., 826-5657), situated in the Mission district hipster zone but without pre-tension. Herbivore has an adventurous selection of meat-free dishes based on Middle Eastern cooking and operates inside a sunny-yellow stucco exterior. The **11:11 Lounge** (1330 Polk St., 885-2652) offers vegan desserts, coffee said to be organic, and countercultural standbys like wheat-grass juice. One of its most appealing offerings is the nicely named angel eyes: a drink made of blended blueberries, banana, coconut, and Rice Dream ice cream. **Valentine's Cafe** (1793 Church St., 285-2257) offers a vegan weekend brunch, including a soy-based favorite called tofu benedict.

Thanks to the strong Asian flavor of San Francisco culture, Asian vegetarian restaurants offer enticing meatless dining. **Bamboo Garden Vegetarian Restaurant** (832 Clement St., 876-0832) is nothing to look at, but its menu is large and varied; oddities like smoky vegetarian "eel" are available, along with tasty vegetarian dim sum. **Golden Era** (572 O'Farrell St., 673-3136) prepares veggie versions of Chinese favorites like sweet and sour soup and Vietnamese dishes like pho noodle soup. **Ananda Fuara** (1298 Market St., 621-1994) serves up spicy vegetarian fare from the Indian subcontinent, at low prices, and features a curry of the day. **Bok Choy Garden** (1820 Clement St., 387-8111) showcases the likes of taro rolls and really good crunchy fried walnuts in sweet and sour sauce. The restaurant prepares food made without onions or garlic, although why anyone would knowingly omit two of the most flavorful and healthful foods on the planet from its cooking surpasses all understanding.

SECRET

VIBRATORS 'N' STUFF

Lubes, fetish wear, naughty videos, and, of course, vibrators for milady are the raison d'être for **Good Vibrations** (1210 Valencia St., 974-8980). Owned by women and very lesbian friendly, the puckishly named shop aims to demystify sex while retaining a touch of whimsy and sense of intimacy. In this admirable goal, it succeeds. Located directly across the street from a public middle school, Good Vibrations' street-level windows are blanked out, but it's a clean, well-lighted place for smut on the inside. Homosexual and heterosexual couples, groups, and singles are all treated with respect and good humor by the smart young staff. Your light whips, your oils, your dildos — they're all here.

More supplies for enhancing those oh-baby moments are on hand — and possibly in hand — at **Stormy Leather** (1158 Howard St., 626-1672). "Ah, the smell of leather and latex in the morning" is a motto of this place, whose advertisements carry the slogan "Forbid Yourself Nothing." It's an omnisexual place where anyone can play or shop. **Leather Men** (1201 Folsom St., 864-7557) is another fine place to stock up on adult play garments. For fetish fashions intended to dazzle and intimidate, the Haight-Ashbury offers Leather Men's sibling store **La Riga** (1391 Haight St., 552-1525), which sells Goth clothing and leather wear. For fetish wear, toys, and assorted accessories, the style mavens at **Dal Jeet's** (1744 Haight St., 752-5610 or 541 Valencia St., 626-9000) promise one-stop shopping in two locations. This is the kind of store Austin Powers would drop a bundle in, right after telling a bird he's been eyeing, "I won't bite . . . much!"

SECRET
VIDEO

❧

Two words: **Le Video**. Stuffed into two Sunset district storefronts, **Le Video** (1231 and 1239 Ninth Ave., 242-2120) has San Francisco's best selection of films on videotape, hands down. Foreign fare, indie work, quirky B-movies, vintage and new porn, genres like science fiction and mystery — and, oh yes, Hollywood movies — are all on hand. Happily, Le Video has a robust selection of documentaries, with special sections devoted to directors Erroll Morris, Nick Broomfield, and the Mayles brothers. There's a section dedicated to Police Cover-Ups and Conspiracy Theories and another to Educational Scare Films, the latter bearing a sign that reads, "Hey, kids, it's trauma time." The stores are fairly well sized (there's an expansive balcony in one), and the staff knows its stuff and is happy to help. The store's Web site, levideo.com, lists info about 45,000 titles. Le Video is highly recommended.

There is **Blockbuster Video** (11 locations) for mainstream movies, and assorted mom and pops, still eking out an existence on street corners or in malls, for pretty much the same thing but with less of a selection. Specialized and alternative fare is also available at **Leather Tongue** (714 Valencia St., 552-2900 or 552-3131), which rents and sells edgy, alternative stuff from a cramped, two-level Mission district space adorned with movie posters. The wonderfully named **Lost Weekend** (1034 Valencia St., 643-3373) is spacious, uncluttered, and well organized, and also has a weird slant. Last time I was there, *Night of the Living Dead* was playing on the TV monitor. There's a rack of filmed-in-S.F. movies, such as Erich Von Stroheim's 1924 feature *Greed*. That's a nice touch, and a rack of staff favorites is another. **Naked Eye News & Video** (533 Haight St., 864-2985) has a great selection of international cinema magazines, tattoo magazines, write it and print it yourself zines, and movies on video, naturally. It's cluttered and a bit disorganized, but intriguing.

For new and old video work by artists, pay a visit to the storefront home of **Artists' Television Access** (992 Valencia St., 824-3890).

ATA screens work by the likes of Bill Viola, perhaps the best-known video artist to come out of the 1970s video-art groundswell, and many more. Political tapes, poetic meditations, personal video diaries, jagged memories of punk rock, and experimental works in many modes are screened regularly. ATA also schedules occasional open screenings for anyone who wants to stop in and show their work.

SECRET

VIETNAMESE

Vietnamese is one of the first fusion cuisines, a happy marriage of Asian ingredients and French accents. This light, healthful, intensely flavorful cuisine is especially well represented in San Francisco, the most heavily Asian-influenced city in the United States.

The city's foodies dote on the **Slanted Door** (584 Valencia St., 861-8032). Chef Charles Phan gives his Vietnamese cuisine a light, California touch and keeps prices surprisingly low. However, while the Slanted Door must be mentioned, truth to tell, it is hardly a secret. Bill Clinton ate there in his last year as president, and the smallish restaurant is always crowded and very noisy, with weeks-long waits for dinner reservations. If you go, try to squeeze in at lunch.

Much less well known, and possibly equally good, is **Thanh Long** (4104 Judah St., 665-1146). Although it is located in the working-class outer Sunset district near the ocean, Thanh Long is upscale, with a large, comfortable main dining room, valet parking, and fairly high prices. The house specialties, which command market prices, are roast crab, drunken crab, and the mouthwatering tamarind crab (a whole Dungeness crab, simmered in sweet-and-sour mélange, with dill and scallions). The ginger-steamed Chilean sea bass is as delicate and flavorful as could be imagined, prepared in a ginger, scallion, and citrus infusion. Jasmine rice stir fried with garlic makes a nice accompaniment to entrees. Thanh Long also has incredible vodka infusions for pre-dinner tippling.

Another Vietnamese place that's not as well known as it should be, perhaps because it's nearly lost in the scrum of Chinese restaurants on outer Geary, is **La Vie** (5830 Geary Blvd., 668-8080). Small and relatively unadorned, with clean lines and discreetly professional service, La Vie is moderately priced and imaginative. The combination appetizer includes crispy imperial rolls, barbequed lemongrass pork, and grilled prawns, served with rice paper, rice noodles, lettuce, and fish sauce. The spicy catfish hot-and-sour soup is made with bean sprouts, tomatoes, pineapple, celery, and mint leaves. La Vie offers several dozen vegetarian dishes, including soups. To drink, there's the Vietnamese beer 33, sweet Vietnamese coffee, and a delightful yellow bean dessert drink with coconut ice cream.

Most San Francisco neighborhoods have Vietnamese places adored by the locals. In the Tenderloin, **Pacific Restaurant-Thai-Binh-Duong No. 2** (337 Jones St., 928-4022) is a favorite of S.F. food critic and restaurateur Patricia Unterman, who champions the Vietnamese noodle dish pho and the spring rolls at this inexpensive neighborhood local. In the inner Richmond district, neighborhood folks grab a quick, tasty, cheap lunch at **Mai's** (316 Clement St., 221-3046), which makes outstanding soups and chili-tinged spicy lemongrass chicken. Just a block away from Mai's is **New Golden Turtle** (308 Fifth Ave., 221-5285). The imperial rolls are nearly a meal in themselves, savory, crispy, and huge, served on a bed of cold noodles, with carrots and heaps of parsley. In the outer Richmond, **Jasmine House**

(2301 Clement St., 668-3382) makes delicious salt and pepper crab and superior garlic noodles that melt in your mouth. Down on Skid Row, **Tu Lan** (8 Sixth St., 626-0927) battles a dreadful location to produce steamy, smoky lunches and dinners at very low prices, served by a friendly, hard-working staff.

The Vietnamese American community is about more than restaurants, of course. Churches, social service agencies, youth programs, and more exist, though they are aimed at residents, not visitors. Americans are beginning to understand that Vietnam is a country, not a war. Vietnam has a San Francisco **consulate** (1700 California St., 922-1577) for those in search of information about the country.

SECRET
VIEWS

Thanks to a happy confluence of sky, water, and hills, San Francisco is one of the world's great cities for spectacular views. It doesn't have Hong Kong's dramatic harbor or Manhattan's forest of island sky-scrapers, but the California sun, the ocean-and-bay fog (which you can watch roll in or peer down on from high places), and closely bunched hills give San Francisco a unique look. Here is a lucky-seven selection of places from which to admire the views; in some cases, you may have the spot to yourself.

Belching tour buses and cars typically make their way to the top of Twin Peaks. The panorama from these high hills is indeed smashing, but the place is too popular for its own good. Almost as high, and far less crowded, is **Tank Hill**, located near the city's geographic center.

You get to it by going to Stanyan and 17th streets, turning left on Belgrave Avenue and walking uphill; the hike keeps a lot of people from going there. Another great spot for panoramic inspiration is **Corona Heights**, which you reach by going to 16th Street and Roosevelt Way and briefly going vertical, walking up to the red rocks. It's a beautiful spot, and it's not crowded. If you have children in tow, you'll be pleased to know it's near the Randall Museum (see Secret Specialty Museums), which is great for kids. You'll catch views of the cityscape and see the slashing diagonal line of Market Street, plus the low ridge of the East Bay hills in the distance. Another fine place to look eastward is the dead end above the Broadway tunnel between **Jones and Taylor Streets**. No through traffic! There's a sweeping view of the city's historic waterfront and of the moon, if it's out, fat and bright and rising over the East Bay hills.

For water views on the east side of town, head out to the end of **Pier 7**. This is a public-access fishing pier with great views of the bay from the far end, where you'll share the space with anglers. On the land end, walkers take their ease on Victorian-style benches and skateboarders practice their moves. Looking westward, you'll take in Telegraph Hill, Coit Tower, and downtown skyscrapers; at night, when the city lights come up, it's magnificent. The cool breezes off the bay are invigorating, too.

For water views on the west side of town, you can look down and back for a commanding view of the Golden Gate Bridge from the wooden deck at **Eagle's Point**, near 32nd Avenue and El Camino del Mar. In sunshine, the bridge is an elegant burnt orange (not gold). At night, the two soaring towers are dramatically lit from underneath. If a giant oceangoing ship is gliding under the bridge's roadway, all the better. The ocean and the long, sandy strand of Ocean Beach are best seen from **Sutro Heights** (48th and Point Lobos avenues). The one-time site of Mayor Adolph Sutro's mansion, Sutro Heights is now a cozy vest-pocket park. On its western and southern sides, you see the beach, the green foliage stream of Golden Gate Park flowing to the sea, the windmills at the park's western edge, and the far-off rising bluff at Fort Funston.

Many high-rise buildings afford breathtaking views and shelter from the elements. The problem is public access, or lack of it, since such structures host company headquarters and other offices. The room near the top of the **Transamerica Pyramid** offers the city's best indoor view, but you need a bona fide reason to get in. I attended a launch party there for the first "Tales of the City" series on PBS and was so taken by the view that I forgot to chat up Olympia Dukakis. As an alternative, take the transparent glass elevators on the outside of the **Westin St. Francis Hotel** (335 Powell St., 397-7000). They're fast, they're sleek, they're free, and they're accessible. You'll think you're in a plane when they take off.

A closing note: there are far too many cameras in the world and people trying to use them, but, yeah, all these places are perfect for taking pictures, too.

SECRET
VINTAGE CLOTHING

In the post-modern world, you can pretty much access anything from the past on a selective basis: haircuts, cars, fridge magnets, old films (used in commercials to sell new personal computers), music, clothing, everything. These days, history is a rummage sale.

Not that the leading vintage clothing shops would want to be associated with anything as déclassé as a rummage sale. While most retro shops have used clothes on offer, some have untouched and unworn items from the past, and some of those items of apparel have a distinctly upscale texture.

For example, **Martini Mercantile** (three S.F. locations) offers swinging party duds for him and her, 1940s style. With two stores in the Haight-Ashbury district and one in North Beach, this snazzily named store is a likely source for something snazzy looking, like wide, short ties and fedoras for guys and swell cocktail dresses for gals. Its North Beach shop (1453 Grant Ave., 362-1944) is somewhat quietly tucked away and not usually crowded. **Crossroads Trading Company** (three S.F. locations) is another vintage shop with an emphasis on a past era's classy attire. Like most vintage shops, Crossroads buys as well as sells retro fashions and is willing to trade clothing as well as accept filthy lucre.

The **Wasteland** (1660 Haight St., 863-3150) is a funkier kind of place with a definition of retro that harkens all the way back to the glittering disco '70s. "All Roads Lead to Where You Are," the store's marketing reminds us. How true. Less philosophical, but perhaps more practical, is **Repeat Performance** (2436 Fillmore St., 563-3123), which sells new and recycled men's and women's clothes, as well as housewares and collectibles, with proceeds benefiting the San Francisco Symphony. At the high end of retro, **Departures from the Past** (2028 Fillmore St., 885-3377) stocks formal wear — think scarves, petticoats, gloves — and overlaps a bit with the costume shop category. Funkier fashions — think bowling shirts and work clothes — can be had at **Captain Jack's** (866 Valencia St., 648-1065), a Mission district store that sells furniture downstairs and men's and women's wear from the '50s through the '80s upstairs. If none of these shops works for you, check out **Retro Fit** (910 Valencia St., 550-1530) and try some new/old threads and a new persona on for size.

SECRET
WALKS AND HIKES

If you like to walk, you're in the right town. At seven miles by seven miles, San Francisco is a small big city, so no place is all that far removed from anyplace else. The hills present a challenge, to be sure, but if you're able bodied and determined, even the steepest slopes are do-able. You'll see a lot by walking around hilly San Francisco — or, as the old joke has it, leaning against San Francisco.

Land's End (Great Hwy. at 48th) provides a bracing blend of city and country. Start at the parking lot overlooking the Cliff House and the ruins of the Sutro Baths, and amble down the well-marked hillside paths, lifting your eyes once in a while to look out to sea. As you round the bend and catch sight of the Golden Gate Bridge, keep going. The dirt path becomes steeper and less well graded. You will share this path with other walkers when you start, but if you keep on through the flowers and up the hillsides, by the time you finish at the Lincoln Park Golf Course, there will be only a handful of people still walking — maybe just you. This path is about one mile long, and the behind-the-scenes nature of the hike will give you a good look at an unpaved part of the city many visitors never see.

Nearby, also on the western edge of town and out behind the Veterans Administration Hospital (43rd and Clement), is a scenic path dedicated to veterans of World War II's Battle of the Bulge. Graded, well marked, and bordered by flowers, it is a fairly steep hillside path that winds down toward the water, and is virtually unused.

In the heart of much-visited Golden Gate Park sits **Stow Lake**, a pretty, manmade body of water swarming with ducks and, along the shores, people. On top of the island in the middle of the lake is tree-fringed Strawberry Hill. A steep grade up the hill keeps most folks off. If you take it, you'll be rewarded with fine views of the city. Although hundreds of people will be hanging out on the shoreline below, you may well have the hilltop to yourself.

For a longer, more strenuous walk, go out to **Glen Canyon Park**, behind the recreation center (Bosworth near Monterey Blvd.) and take the footpath. The path winds through fragrant eucalyptus trees to a ravine in the woods. Wood-plank bridges pass over a marsh and through tall grass. You get plenty of fresh air on this walk, and it's rarely crowded; many people, even locals, don't know it's there.

Downtown has a number of interesting places that are best discovered on foot. The stairways through residential neighborhoods are especially rewarding. Most people drive up to Coit Tower, for example; if you walk, climbing the concrete **Greenwich Street steps** and pausing as needed to catch your breath, you'll see more, passing neatly kept cottages and catching views of downtown. The **Filbert Street steps**, made of planks and flanked by greenery, run between Coit Tower and Sansome Street on the eastern slope of Telegraph Hill; keep an eye peeled for the wild parrots that live in the Grace Marchant Gardens there. The **Lyon Street steps**, beginning between Broadway and Green Street, lead into a neatly tended English garden and give you a good look at the edge of the Presidio. The **Vulcan Street steps**, off Market Street near 17th Street, are one long block of concrete steps between Ord and Levant streets away from the tumult of upper Market Street.

Much more celebrated, and still fun, is **Macondray Lane**, near Leavenworth between Union and Green streets, which was the model for the fictional Barbary Lane in Armistead Maupin's *Tales of the City* books. Macondray Lane has an arched entryway at the western end and a plank stairway at the eastern end, and is lined with pretty cottages and flowers. The **Harry Street steps**, between Laidley and Beacon streets, are a Noe Valley secret. More than 200 concrete and wood steps take you past rustic cottages, and the Victorian-era Bell Mansion is close by.

For more information, contact the **San Francisco Convention and Visitors Bureau** (391-2000 or www.sfvisitor.org), or go to the Visitors Center in Hallidie Plaza and pick up a free brochure with map called *San Francisco Walking Tours*. The **San Francisco Public Library's City Guides** (557-4266) lead free guided tours — 26 tours in all — keyed to the Gold Rush, Art Deco buildings, and so on. Tours, lasting up to two hours, are led by volunteer guides trained by the library. There are also many independent guides and tour companies that sell themed walks in Chinatown, North Beach, and elsewhere. Information is available from the SFCVB (see above).

Lastly, this public service announcement: when walking the streets of San Francisco, remember what your mother told you, and look both ways before crossing. It wouldn't hurt to stay on the curb for a few seconds, either. In 2000, some thirty pedestrians were killed by cars in S.F. Some were jaywalking; others were hit by red-light runners. Stay awake and don't become a statistic.

SECRET

WATERFRONT

The water made San Francisco. This city had the greatest port on the west coast of the Americas until after World War II, and the city proper was the first great Pacific coast city in the Americas. These days, the port is used mostly for recreation and developers' real-estate plays. The shoreline, if not the city's long-gone cargo shipping, has been revived in recent years with the demolition of the hideous double-decker Embarcadero Freeway in 1991 and the opening of Pacific Bell Park for baseball's San Francisco Giants in 2000. Not all the great things about the waterfront are monumental, however, and you can find low-key pleasures all along it.

Look closely to find **The Ramp** (855 China Basin, 621-2378). It is a well-known waterside beer and barbeque joint to locals, but for visitors it may as well be in another city. No easily visible sign marks this spot, which you reach by crossing a parking lot off a lightly trafficked road. Sunny and warm, with a patio used for dancing on weekends, the Ramp pours good draft beers and serves basic food; the curly fries are so curly, they're like corkscrews. From the Ramp's patio, you can look out at pleasure craft anchored in the marina and hear the bay water lap at the shore.

Before World War II, the **Ferry Building** (Market and the Embarcadero), designed by architect A. Page Brown, was the busiest ferry terminal in the United States. Water traffic sank fast when the Bay Bridge and the Golden Gate Bridge opened in 1936 and 1937, respectively. Inside the becalmed Ferry Building, along the central ramp heading upstairs, are big wall murals depicting the peoples of the Pacific Rim basin in native dress, working in fields and factories amid representations of native flora and fauna. The paintings are kitschy and outdated, but they're endearing somehow. You have to hope they're in the plans for the Ferry Building, which is closed for a $70-million upgrade in 2001 and 2002.

More history is available underfoot, thanks to the **Historic Interpretative Signage Project** along the Embarcadero, which has embedded plaques in the sidewalk to mark important spots in S.F. history and share important thoughts. "Men are very fond of proving their steadfast adherence to nonsense," harrumphed "Edward Beale, 1842." Tell it, Ed. Near the Beale plaque, you can stand on the Embarcadero at Harrison Street and take a gander — look up, up — at the immense, slate-gray Bay Bridge. Overshadowed by the glamorous Golden Gate Bridge, this span is nevertheless enormous and enormously busy; you can appreciate its immensity from this spot.

On the water side of the Embarcadero stands **Red's Java House** (Pier 28, no listed phone), a beer, burger, and coffee shack that's been there since about 1920. Red's, a favorite of construction workers, is impossibly cheap and open for breakfast and lunch only. You order at the counter. I stopped in for a Bud and a cheeseburger and asked them to hold the pickles. "No pickles? No problem," replied the cheery order taker, who brought the grub to my table two minutes later. Red's is not the only "java house" on the waterfront, but it is the one worth patronizing.

While passing by the tourist tackiness of much of Fisherman's Wharf, don't forget to admire the impressively large, arched entrances to the old finger piers, which were essential to the workaday port; they are done in Gothic revival style, and many are handsome. For a different kind of beauty, go to the end of the jetty at the St. Francis Yacht Club, west of Fort Mason Center, and sit down by the **Wave Organ**. Created in the mid-1980s by artist Peter Richards, this structure

resembling an ancient stone amphitheater incorporates several dozen pipes that amplify the gurgle and bubble of bay waters, creating a naturally musical sound.

On the ocean side, the famous **Cliff House** is a magnet for huge, fuming tour buses whose drivers allow the engines to idle endlessly after the vehicles disgorge their passengers in search of keepsakes. The present Cliff House is an architectural mish-mash, an undistinguished successor to fabulous Victorian predecessors that looked like big layer cakes. Mark Twain dined in an earlier Cliff House, and San Franciscans considered the place quite classy as recently as the 1930s, when a book hopefully entitled *Where to Sin in San Francisco* rhapsodized: "From your table on the very edge of the United States, stirring sights are to be seen. The everlasting pageantry of sea and sky. The unending cavalcade of sea rovers steaming in and out of the Golden Gate: great liners, tramp steamers, fishing boats. And in the sky, the Clippers winging off to the Far East."

The ocean liners and Pan American Flying Clipper planes are gone, but the pageantry of sea and sky remains. If you're at the Cliff House, go out back and down the stairs, and check out the **Camera Obscura** (1090 Point Lobos Ave., 750-0415). In a 1949 camera-shaped building that overlooks the water, you can look at live images of sea and sky in a darkened room with a device used in Leonardo de Vinci's time. If it's foggy, the manager shut the place down. Price: $1. Or go about 75 feet and pop into the **Musée Mecanique** (1090 Point Lobos Ave., 386-1170). There, you can squint into a 90-year-old stereoscope and view the ruins of San Francisco during the 1906 earthquake and fire in 3-D. For a happier experience, see the peep-show "What the Belly Dancer Does on Her Day Off." Price: 25 cents.

SECRET
WE NEVER CLOSE

You've been having such a good time that you don't want to mess it up by going to sleep. So you're staying up all night. Hey, *Secret San Francisco* understands; *Secret San Francisco* has been there. You want some food. Maybe you need some medication, or you have an irresistible urge to do your clothes in a 24-hour coin laundry. No problem.

In the always-lively Castro district, you can get breakfast any time you want it at the **Bagdad Cafe** (2295 Market St., 621-4434), and if you want it with turkey sausage, well, you can get that, too. The young, gay patrons and staff are likely to be bouncing off the walls at any hour. Retro decor and diner food rule at **Sparky's** (242 Church St., 626-8666), and come about 3 a.m., it will seem like retro on Mars in this quintessential nighthawks' nest. To find out just how weird weird can be, visit the **Video Cafe** (21st and Geary, 387-3999), where movies play on TV monitors non-stop and low riders who have worked up major appetites partying at the beach come in and want to be served *now*. At **Cafe Mason** (320 Mason St., 544-0320), in the downtown theater district, the scene is pretty much the same as at the other spots: American diner food, retro decor, nocturnal characters.

Fudging the We Never Close definition — alright, temporarily abandoning that definition — enables me to mention the **Grubstake** (1525 Pine St., 673-8268), which does close, but not until 4 a.m. In the meantime, it feeds the late-night bar crowd and gay street hustlers in Polk Gulch. Half of the Grubstake is crammed into a former railroad car from the Key System, which used to link the East Bay and San Francisco; the other half spills into a more or less normal building.

You pay $1.50 for a cup of coffee, but they keep refilling it, and you can order either standard-issue greasy spoon fare or some not-bad Portuguese meat dishes put on the menu by the Portuguese owner. Last time I was there, an out-of-costume drag queen explained, in a bass voice, that he didn't have a show to do that night, which was good because it takes two hours to put on the dress and all the make-up and, anyway, he was gearing up for a holiday in London.

Yuct Lee (1300 Stockton St., 982-6020) isn't strictly We Never Close, either, as this redoubtable Chinese place shuts down at 3 a.m. But until then, it's the best late-night place in town. It's cheap, with really good food that is far preferable to the food in places that actually don't close.

Should you be in need of household appliances or wilted produce south of the midnight hour, **Cala Foods** (seven S.F. locations), a locally owned supermarket chain, keeps stores open all night. For a medical emergency, dire need for condoms, or dire need for coffee ice cream, some **Walgreen's** pharmacies are open 24 hours, including those in the Castro (1333 Castro St., 826-8998) and the outer Richmond (25 Point Lobos Ave., 386-0706).

And your clothes — where to do laundry? Think **Highlander** (445 Judah St., no listed phone), with its old but operating washers and dryers, soda machine, graffiti-covered pay phone, linoleum floors, and murky yellow light. It's open.

SECRET
WHATZIT

What's a Whatzit? Beats me. This is just a category I invented for places I think are cool that don't fit into any other category I could dream up — places like the following:

Paxton Gate (824 Valencia St., 824-1872) is your one-stop shop for dead stuffed mice. Yes, the taxidermist has been hard at work in this curious retail outlet, which also sells high-end gardening tools. Displays of stuffed mice in costume — dressed as religious figures, as the devil, as a rather scary-looking vampire — are displayed and offered for sale. The shop also has a collection of other dead critters preserved for you, such as butterflies and large beetles. **Happy Trails** (1615 Haight St., 431-7232) is a happier place. No dark images here: just a quirky, funny inventory of rubber chickens, Elvis kitsch, candy cigarettes, and other retro stuff. **Howling Bull Syndicate** (826 Valencia St., 282-0339), sibling to a similar store in Tokyo, is a retail outlet that sells strange collectables like Ultraman toys, as well as punk and other rock CDs, and zines such as *Tattoo Revue* and *Tokyo Pop*.

Quantity Postcards (1441 Grant Ave., 788-4455) also displays weird stuff around its small retail space: big papier-mâché heads, flying saucer motifs, guess-your-weight scales. But it sells only one thing: postcards. Not your gauzy shots of Alamo Park Victorian houses or San Francisco cable cars, but retro orange-crate art from the Great Depression era, 3-D Christs, pop stars like the Everly Brothers, the Beatles, and the young Rolling Stones, and reproductions from pulp magazines. I've shopped in this place for years and never knew it had a name. There's no sign, so look closely. This is just a great place. And it's cheap, with nothing over a buck. Most of the cards cost far less.

Then there's **Helmand** (430 Broadway, 362-0641), an elegant Afghani restaurant unaccountably located amid the sleaze and noise of Broadway. Even in a restaurant-mad town like San Francisco, Afghani restaurants are not thick on the ground. Beautifully spiced meat dishes, dollops of cooling yogurt, and quiet and correct service with no forced touch of the exotic distinguish Helmand. It's a North Beach neighborhood favorite. Try the pumpkin ravioli and anything with lamb.

SECRET
WINE
⚜

California produces 90 percent of all the wine made in the United States, and the state's premier wine regions, Napa Valley and Sonoma Valley, are just an hour's drive north of San Francisco. You would expect the city to be a center of wine drinking and wine wisdom, and, sure enough, it is.

Wine is at the heart of an interesting food and recreation empire run by S.F. politician Gavin Newsom and oil heir Billy Getty. The business partners own **PlumpJack Cafe** (3127 Fillmore St., 563-4755), a small, casually elegant place for robust California food that has a strong wine list. It figures: Newsom and Getty also own PlumpJack Winery in Napa Valley and **PlumpJack Wines** (3201 Fillmore St., 346-6837 or 346-9870), just down the block from the cafe. The wine store sells a fine selection at reasonable prices, and it is especially good at taking the intimidation factor out of buying wine. It also sells wine online at www.plumpjack.com.

Another S.F. wine shop whose managers gladly share their knowledge of wine and offer good value is **Wine Impression** (3461 California St., 221-9463 or 221-5505), located in the Laurel Village shopping complex near the shopping zone along Sacramento Street. Wine Impressions hosts tasting events and has a tasting bar, and is especially good on Italian wines. The O'Flynn family of San Francisco operates another of my favorites, **California Wine Merchant** (3237 Pierce St., 567-0646), which specializes in unique California wines, such as Silver Oak Cabernet Sauvignon from the Alexander Valley, and the smooth and expensive Paradigm Cabernet Sauvignon from Oakville. The shop is small and stocks only first-rate wines. The **Ashbury Market** (205 Frederick St., 566-3134) has a well-chosen selection of French and California wines in a space shared with a deli and neighborhood mom and pop grocery.

Every serious restaurant in the city is serious about wine, excepting maybe small ethnic and neighborhood places. **Greens** (Fort Mason Center, Building A, 771-6222) is a leader in matching wine with food. This vegetarian gourmet restaurant is owned and operated by the San Francisco Zen Center, but has little Zen austerity about it, stocking some 500 brands of elegant wine, most from California and the Pacific Northwest. **Elka's** (900 Bush St., 928-1888) has wine tastings on Wednesdays from 5:30 to 7:30 p.m., with free hors d'oeuvres. **Cafe Niebaum-Coppola** (916 Kearny St., 291-1700), in the Sentinel flatiron building, is a sparkling Parisian bistro with a fine selection of champagne and other wines, including vintages made by the cafe's co-owner, film director Francis Ford Coppola. The cafe's wine-tasting bar offers some 100 wines. **Eos** (901 Cole St., 566-3063), an adventurous Asian fusion restaurant, also operates a fine wine bar. The wait for chef Arnold Wong's creations can be lengthy, so the wine bar is a good place to try a new wine, talk, and relax.

The wine bar phenomenon is not all that phenomenal in San Francisco, perhaps because so many restaurants and markets provide so many choices when it comes to wine. However, several worthy freestanding wine bars offer wines by the glass or bottle, along with food ranging from snacks to light meals. **Hayes & Vine** (377 Hayes St., 626-5301) is a fun wine bar in the Hayes Valley high-culture zone near Davies Symphony Hall and the War Memorial Opera House; it's perfect for pre- or post-performance sipping. The **London Wine Bar** (415 Sansome St., 788-4811) is a popular after-work meeting place for people from the surrounding financial district. Open since 1974 in a swellegant brick building, it claims to be the first wine bar in America. Cheese plates and hors d'oeuvres complement wines by the glass. Try to get into one of the comfortable dark-wood booths. It's closed on weekends.

If you're heading out of town to the wine country, check first with **Napa Valley Visitors Information** (707-226-7455) and **Sonoma Valley Visitors Information** (707-996-1090). Napa is better known, and there are many good wineries there, but Napa is also overrun and many wineries charge for tastings. Personally, I prefer lesser-known and less-crowded Sonoma, which also makes some remarkable wines and is lower key than its famous neighbor. Sonoma also retains some of its historic apple orchards and dairy farms, giving it a rounded agricultural quality.

THE SECRET FUTURE

No tour guide can be definitively comprehensive, especially when the aim is to uncover those hidden places that have previously escaped notice. Undoubtedly, some worthwhile attractions have remained hidden even from our best efforts to ferret them out.

In the interest of our own self-improvement, we ask readers to let us know of the places they've unearthed that they believe warrant inclusion in future editions of *Secret San Francisco*. If we use your suggestion, we'll send you a free copy on publication. Please contact us at the following address:

Secret San Francisco
c/o ecw press

2120 Queen Street East, Suite 200
Toronto, Ontario, Canada m4e 1e2

Or e-mail us at: ecw_info@on.aibn.com

PHOTO SITES

SUBJECT INDEX

Books and Literary Interests

Fairs/Festivals/Celebrations

Fashion/Clothing

ALPHABETICAL INDEX